What Now?

Transform Your Bible in a Year
Reading From Trivial Pursuit to
The Pursuit of God

———

Kristopher K. Barnett

What Now? Transform Your Bible in a Year Reading From Trivial Pursuit
to The Pursuit of God
Copyright © 2011 by Kristopher K. Barnett

Koozzz Publishing
Mount Vernon, Ohio 43050

Cover photograph by Koozzz Photographic

ISBN-13: 978-0-9830760-2-5
ISBN-10: 0-9830760-2-2

Library of Congress Control Number: 2011940453

DEDICATION

The Bible tells the story of family. The story starts with Adam's family and continues past Mary and Joseph's clan. On every page we discover the family of Israel and eventually we come to the incredible realization that we are a part of that family, God's family. This book is dedicated to my families:

The church family at East Pickens Baptist Church, they served as guinea pigs for this project and encouraged its completion.

My little family, we have experienced growth and joy during this project. Each member of my family inspires me each day, particularly, the Princess who edits my words and encourages my heart.

The greater family of God, my prayer is that this work will strengthen the church universal. I firmly believe that the word of God must be read and lived in order for the family of God to experience and express the presence of God.

My Heavenly Father, He gave His Son so that I could be a part of His family. I pray that this work will introduce some to the Father's family and help those already in the family to live like they belong.

TABLE OF CONTENTS

PREFACE

Unlike most writers, I did not set out to write a book. In fact, I had finished half of it before I realized what was taking shape. This book started as a pastoral project, directed toward a need I sensed in my own congregation. Let me tell you how it took shape.

As 2010 approached, I sensed the Lord leading me to challenge my congregation to read through the Bible in a year. I researched different reading plans. I looked for something that would challenge Christians who read the Bible regularly, yet be accessible to Christians unfamiliar with the Bible. The reading plan, included in this book, that offered selections each day from the Old Testament, New Testament, Psalms, and Proverbs seemed to offer the diversity I sought.

After selecting the reading plan, I looked for resources to assist the members of my congregation who accepted the challenge to read through the Bible in a year. From personal experience and observation, I knew that most approached Bible reading for information rather than transformation. I wanted my congregation to move beyond simply reading the word of God and experience the joy of living out the word of God. The search for application based resources yielded little fruit.

Disappointed in the meager results of my search, I decided that I might be able to provide something for my congregation. So, the last week of December in 2009, I started writing application oriented questions for publication in our church bulletin. Throughout 2010, I continued writing these questions for the upcoming week's Bible reading. Those questions provided the foundation for What Now?

Interestingly enough, the project almost died an early death. About three months into writing these application questions, I started wondering if anyone utilized them. I had invested several hours on these questions each week and this fear suddenly crept over me. I wondered if the copies sat unused on the church's welcome desk each week. I didn't see piles of them in the pews on Sunday morning but perhaps the custodian disposed of them before I arrived on Monday to save my fragile ego.

I asked around to test my theory. I spoke to the Wednesday night Bible study and prayer group. This group prayed fervently and studied feverishly. I knew they would give an honest reply. When I confessed my doubts about the usefulness of these application questions, they adamantly reassured me that members used the questions. The couple that headed up our welcome ministry pointed out that when the questions didn't make it to the welcome desk, people asked about them. (Some even asked passionately!) This encouraged me to continue and saved the project you hold in your hands.

The project almost died a second time when God provided an unexpected call in my life. Midway through 2010, the Lord led me to transition from pastoral to academic ministry. The day I announced to my congregation that I was leaving to teach at Anderson University, the first question that several church members asked was, "Will you still provide the questions for us?" By this point, I was already committed, so I pledged to finish what I had started. Around the same time, an idea started formulating in my mind.

Somewhere around the middle of the year, just before I transitioned to educational ministry, a thought occurred to me. If the people in my church appreciated and utilized a resource like this one, perhaps other followers of Christ could benefit from this material as well. Having done the research prior, I knew that no such resource existed. So, I took the idea to a publisher.

After a slow and meandering journey, I discovered that the most likely publisher for this project was not interested. At this point, the project almost died a third time. But, in the midst of rejection, I discovered Jeff Kusner at Koozzz Publishing. Jeff, the operator of the site oneyearbibleonline.com, was new to publishing and expressed enthusiasm for this project the first time I inquired through email. We discussed different means to get the resource in the hands of Bible readers. After considering a few options, we determined that a print copy with space for journaling would be the best. That decision led to the product that you hold in your hands.

So, What Now? comes to you as a simple project, born from pastoral ministry and designed for practical application. James 1:22 reminds us, "Do not merely listen to the word, and so deceive yourselves. Do what it says." In order to obey this admonition, we must recognize the awe-inspiring power of God's Word. Hebrews 4:12 reveals, "For the word of God is living and active. Sharper than any double-edged sword, it penetrates even to dividing soul and spirit, joints and marrow; it judges the thoughts and attitudes of the heart." I challenge you to let the Word do its work in your life. I hope and pray that What Now? opens your soul and spirit to the Word of God, enabling the Surgeon's scalpel to rearrange your life according to His desire.

INTRODUCTION

"Tips for the Journey"

I am excited that you have made the commitment to read through the Bible. God has revealed Himself to His people through His Word. I know that He will speak to you as you read His Word. As you begin this journey, I'd like to offer a few tips.

Establish a consistent time for reading God's Word. Although this reading plan will likely only take 15-20 minutes a day, those minutes will not materialize without intentionality and planning. Select a time and a place for reading God's Word. Perhaps you function well early in the morning, or you are a night owl. Make sure that the time you select works best with your natural rhythms of life. In addition, let your friends and family know about your plan and ask them to help you protect the time that you establish.

Select a translation you can read. If you cannot read the translation of the Bible you own, find a different translation! God did not give His Word to His people in order to keep it distant and foreign. He gave His Word so that His people could discover Him. Find a translation that enables you to encounter God.

Connect your reading of God's Word to prayer. Invite the Holy Spirit to direct you and teach you. Scripture reading minus prayer is hollow and empty. Scripture reading with prayer is illuminated and informed. One specific suggestion here is to learn to pray Scripture. When you read a prayer or praise in Scripture, use those words as your own exclamation to God.

Involve others in your journey. Although we typically think of reading as a solitary endeavor, we should include others. First, it is invaluable to find individuals who will hold you accountable in your efforts. Second, you can involve others by sharing with friends, family and co-workers the insights that God has given you. Finally, this might be a great opportunity to start or continue a family devotion time. For example, your family could read the assigned reading from Psalms or Proverbs each day at mealtime or at night before bedtime.

Be prepared for spiritual attacks. Our adversary, the devil, is antagonistic toward anything that might lead to spiritual growth. Bible reading is the most important factor for spiritual development. Therefore, you should be prepared for the obstacles and road blocks that Satan will launch as you begin this journey. Don't be surprised when you struggle to find time for Bible reading or you are faced with challenging circumstances in your life. In fact, you should expect it.

Keep pace but practice grace. Be disciplined in your reading. However, recognize that there will be days when your schedule goes awry and you will fail to spend time in the Word. As noted above, Satan wants to trip you up. One of his favorite tools is guilt, which he often employs to lead believers away from the study of Scripture. So, if you miss a couple of days reading the Word, Satan will plant this lie in your thoughts, "I'm so far behind I can never catch up." Do you see how Satan wins with this lie? Rather than continuing to enjoy God's Word at a slower pace, you completely lose the benefits of consistent Bible reading. Don't buy the lie.

Read the Bible. This seems so obvious that it shouldn't be necessary. However, from personal experience and observation I know that it is needed. When you find yourself rushing to spend time with God, resist the temptation to jump to the questions and skip reading the Bible. The questions in this book do not stand alone. They depend on the Scripture reading. If you must choose one or the other, choose Scripture every time!

I hope that these tips benefit you as you begin this journey. I know that God will speak into your life as you listen to His voice.

10

JANUARY

GENESIS 1:1-2:25	JAN
MATTHEW 1:1-2:12	**1**
PSALM 1:1-6	
PROVERBS 1:1-6	

Application:

1. Take note of the evidence of God's creation that you see today. Spend some time worshipping God for his creative power.

2. How does the reality that you are made in the image of God impact your life?

3. How does Genesis 2 impact your understanding of marriage?

4. How does the beginning of Matthew relate to the beginning of Genesis?

5. When are you tempted to listen to the counsel of the wicked?

_____

_____

_____

_____

_____

_____

_____

GENESIS 3:1-4:26	JAN
MATTHEW 2:13-3:6	**2**
PSALM 2:1-12	
PROVERBS 1:7-9	

Application:

1. How do you see the impact of the fall in the world today? How do you see the impact of the fall in your life today?
2. What can you discover about Satan's methods of temptation in Genesis 3? How does Satan use those same methods against you?
3. How did the birth of Christ fulfill OT prophecy?

_____

_____

_____

_____

_____

_____

_____

_____

GENESIS 5:1-7:24 MATTHEW 3:7-4:11 PSALM 3:1-8 PROVERBS 1:10-19	JAN **3**

Application:

1. How does our society resemble that of Noah?
2. If God were looking for one righteous person today, would he look to you? How can you adjust your actions and/or attitudes to reflect God's righteousness?
3. Have you followed the Lord's example in baptism? If not, talk to your pastor about publicly expressing your faith through baptism.
4. How does the temptation of Jesus differ from the fall of man in Genesis 3? What can you learn from the distinctions?

_____

_____

_____

_____

_____

_____

_____

GENESIS 8:1-10:32 **MATTHEW 4:12-25** **PSALM 4:1-8** **PROVERBS 1:20-23**	JAN **4**

Application:

1. How does the "rainbow covenant" offer hope today?
2. Noah was a "righteous man", but yet he was drunk in his tent. How does this apparent contradiction impact your understanding of grace?
3. Jesus promised the disciples that He would make them Fisher's of Men. How can God use you as a Fisher of Men?
4. The Psalmist often cries out to God in frustration and desperation. Do your prayers reveal that level of honesty? If not, take some time today to express your true feelings to God.

_____

_____

_____

_____

_____

_____

GENESIS 11:1-13:4 MATTHEW 5:1-26 PSALM 5:1-12 PROVERBS 1:24-28	JAN 5

Application:

1. How is the arrogance of man reflected in the Tower of Babel also reflected in the technology of contemporary culture?
2. Is God calling you to take a leap of faith like Abram?
3. Who could use a ray of light from your life today?
4. What can you do to salt the world?
5. Praise God for the moments in your life when he blessed your path because you heeded his directions.

_____

_____

_____

_____

_____

_____

_____

_____

_____

GENESIS 13:5-15:21 MATTHEW 5:27-48 PSALM 6:1-10 PROVERBS 1:29-33	JAN **6**

Application:

1. Have you experienced times in your life when you were shafted by a "Lot" but God provided for you anyway? Thank God for those events in your life.

2. Consider the honesty of Abram's dialogue with God in Genesis 15. Is your relationship with God such that you can honestly share your heart? What are you holding back from God?

3. Does Jesus' teaching in the Sermon on the Mount convict you for living by the letter of the law (thou shall not kill) and ignoring the Spirit of the Law (thou shall not hate)? What can you do to embrace the Spirit of the Law?

4. Have waywardness and complacency ever led you to make poor choices in life? Ask God to help you to see the value in each daily choice. Pray that God will grant you wisdom in all decisions.

_____

_____

_____

_____

_____

GENESIS 16:1-18:15 MATTHEW 6:1-24 PSALM 7:1-17 PROVERBS 2:1-5	JAN 7

Application:

1. Sarai proposed a short-term solution for the couple's childlessness. Abram trusted Sarai's plan over God's long-range plan. In what areas are you tempted to short-cut God's plans for your life?

2. Following God requires deliberate and decisive obedience (i.e. - circumcision for Abraham). What sort of deliberate and decisive obedience does God desire from you today?

3. Have you ever laughed at God? What was the result of the laughter?

4. Do you perform acts of righteousness for the benefit of man or God? Ask the Holy Spirit to clarify those motives to you and help you make those motives pure.

5. How are you investing in eternal things?

GENESIS 18:16-19:38 MATTHEW 6:25-7:14 PSALM 8:1-9 PROVERBS 2:6-15	JAN **8**

Application:

1. Abraham's interaction with God concerning Sodom and Gomorrah points to the value of praying for others. Who needs your intercession today?
2. What areas of your life are taking priority over the kingdom? What can you do to prioritize those areas properly?
3. Do you have a problem with worry? Worry is a sin, not a bad-habit or an acceptable part of your personality. Trust God and hand over your worry.
4. Sing a praise song to God, worshipping His majestic name.

GENESIS 20:1-22:24 MATTHEW 7:15-29 PSALM 9:1-12 PROVERBS 2:16-22	JAN 9

Application:

1. Abraham again lies and calls his wife his sister. This story reveals that each individual has a tendency toward specific sins. What temptations snare you most regularly? Ask for God's forgiveness and assistance in avoiding those temptations.

2. In her greatest distress, Hagar discovered that God had not forgotten her. Perhaps you are facing great distress today, cry out to God and discover His presence. If you are not facing distress today, thank God for those times when he rescued you in the past.

3. What does your fruit reveal about your faith?

GENESIS 23:1-24:51 MATTHEW 8:1-17 PSALM 9:13-20 PROVERBS 3:1-6	JAN **10**

Application:

1. The love story of Isaac and Rebekah is touching. It is even more powerful when we consider the hand of God working to bring the two together through the prayer of Abraham's servant. Celebrate God's providential work in bringing you into your current situation.

2. Matthew reveals Jesus' power over illness and disease. Do you trust Jesus with your health? While I believe that God provides doctors and medicine for the benefit of man, we must always trust God as the Master Healer.

3. Are you acknowledging (trusting) God in all your ways or are you leaning on your own understanding? Remember, this involves the "small" decisions as well as the "big" decisions.

_____

_____

_____

_____

_____

_____

GENESIS 24:52-26:16 MATTHEW 8:18-34 PSALM 10:1-15 PROVERBS 3:7-8	JAN **11**

Application:

1. When Abraham died he owned only the land where he and Sarah were buried. What does this teach you about persevering faith? In what areas do you trust God for the unseen?

2. Isaac perpetuates the legacy of deceit passed on from Abraham when he claims that Rebekah is his sister. Which sinful habits are you passing on to your family?

3. Some offered Jesus excuses while others followed. What excuses prohibit you from following Christ in faith?

4. Jesus called the disciples men of little faith. How would he describe your faith?

GENESIS 26:17-27:46 MATTHEW 9:1-17 PSALM 10:16-18 PROVERBS 3:9-10	JAN **12**

Application:

1. The patriarchs often built altars to commemorate God-moments in their life. What does Isaac commemorate? What God-moments do you need to commemorate?

2. Isaac's family reveals a great deal of dysfunction. Jacob and Rebekah plotted and schemed, Esau fumed and fought. What dysfunction are you perpetuating in your family?

3. Jesus asked, "Why do you entertain evil thoughts in your hearts?" (Matthew 9:4). Does his question convict you? If so, what about?

4. "I desire mercy, not sacrifice." (Matthew 9:13) Pray that God will help you understand and practice this in your life.

5. The Psalmist points out that God is the defender of the fatherless and oppressed. How are you joining Him in this role?

_____

_____

_____

_____

_____

_____

| GENESIS 28:1-29:35
MATTHEW 9:18-38
PSALM 11:1-7
PROVERBS 3:11-12 | JAN
13 |

Application:

1. How does God's revelation in Jacob's dream shape Jacob's faith in the years to come? How has God's revelation shaped your life?

2. "The girl is not dead, but asleep." (Matthew 9:24) Jesus calls you to believe the unbelievable. He calls you to trust Him when life is at its worst. Where are you having trouble believing the unbelievable in your life?

3. Pray that God will raise up workers for the harvest in your city.

4. Do you believe that the discipline of the Lord reveals His love? How has God's discipline revealed his love in your life?

_____

_____

_____

_____

_____

_____

_____

| GENESIS 30:1-31:16
MATTHEW 10:1-23
PSALM 12:1-8
PROVERBS 3:13-15 | JAN
14 |

Application:

1. Jacob, the deceiver, is deceived by his father-in-law. The two con-men go back and forth for awhile. Sometimes the sins that most aggravate us in others are the sins that we recognize from our own lives. Is this true in your life? Confess these sins to God and ask Him to help you overcome them.

2. After Jesus asked his disciples to pray for workers for the harvest, He sends his disciples to the harvest field. Where has Jesus sent you? How are you harvesting in your sphere of influence: your job, your school, your family, etc.?

3. The Psalmist lamented the absence of the godly. His cry implies a longing for fellowship with other believers. Thank God for the church family that He has given you. Call someone today and tell them how much you appreciate their presence.

_____

_____

_____

_____

_____

GENESIS 31:17-32:12 MATTHEW 10:24-11:6 PSALM 13:1-6 PROVERBS 3:16-18	JAN **15**

Application:

1. Jacob cries out to God as he returns to the Promised Land. God told him to return but with Esau closing in on him, Jacob is terrified. When have you cried out in terror during times of obedience?

2. Sometimes we feel unimportant or insignificant but God knows the number of hairs on our head. Thank Him for His knowledge of you!

3. What must you do to lose your life for the sake of Jesus?

4. "But I trust in your unfailing love." (Psalm 13:5) Perhaps today you need to trust in his unfailing love. Commit to him the situations that you are wrestling with and trust his love.

GENESIS 32:13-34:31 MATTHEW 11:7-30 PSALM 14:1-7 PROVERBS 3:19-20	JAN **16**

Application:

1. How are your wrestling skills? Jacob would not let go of God until he received a blessing. Are you willing to hold on to God with that type of fervor? Do you have any scars, like Jacob's limp, from holding on to God? Share the story of your scars with someone today who needs encouragement in their faith.

2. El Elohe Israel - Mighty is the God of Israel! When you are weary remember, the God of Israel is your Mighty God, too!

3. How does your life reflect the yoke/teaching of Christ?

4. Jesus calls you to come to Him and find rest for your weary soul. Take some time today to rest in the Father's presence.

5. Have you ever considered the vastness of the seas? God's knowledge created the murky depths. Meditate on God's creative power and incredible knowledge!

_____

_____

_____

_____

_____

GENESIS 35:1-36:43 MATTHEW 12:1-21 PSALM 15:1-5 PROVERBS 3:21-26	JAN **17**

Application:

1. Bethel means the place where God revealed Himself. Where is your Bethel? Where does God most frequently reveal Himself?

2. Jesus constantly battled the Pharisees. Jesus was a square peg who refused to be crammed into their round hole of religiosity. How do you attempt to cram Jesus into your expectations of religion?

3. Look closely at Psalm 15. The Psalmist describes several characteristics of those whose walk is blameless. Is your walk blameless? Use the characteristics in the Psalm as a self-test. (Am I righteous? Do I speak the truth? Do I slander?, etc.) In the areas where your actions are not blameless, ask for God's forgiveness and help.

_____

_____

_____

_____

_____

| GENESIS 37:1-38:30 MATTHEW 12:22-45 PSALM 16:1-11 PROVERBS 3:27-32 | JAN 18 |

Application:

1. Joseph's brothers reveal the danger of allowing jealousy and resentment to fester. They are willing to kill or sell their brother. Against whom are you allowing jealousy and anger to fester in your soul?

2. The story of Judah and Tamar is a scandalous excursion. The narrative reveals the hypocrisy and immorality of Judah. It is also telling that Jesus came from the lineage of Judah (the Lion of the Tribe of Judah). If your past is checkered and the branches of your family tree are scandalous, thank God today because He can overcome your past!

3. While Jesus condemns the Pharisees for their lack of fruit, He warns that man will be held accountable for every word that they have spoken. How will your words stand up to the scrutiny of God's judgment?

4. Praise God today for the moments that He has been your refuge.

GENESIS 39:1-41:16 MATTHEW 12:46-13:23 PSALM 17:1-15 PROVERBS 3:33-35	JAN **19**

Application:

1. Over and over the writer of Genesis reveals that the Lord was with Joseph. While the circumstances scream of God's absence, we are reminded of God's presence. Are you facing circumstances that indicate God is absent? Trust that God's presence never changes!

2. "When two full years had passed..." (Genesis 41:1) This chronological notation is easily overlooked. Joseph languished in prison for two more years due to the forgetfulness of the cupbearer. How are you currently waiting on God? Remember Joseph's example of patience in the prison and more importantly, remember God's faithfulness!

3. How is your soil? How are you cultivating the seeds that God places in your life?

4. The Lord "blesses the home of the righteous." (Proverbs 3:33) What can you do to make your home a place of righteousness?

GENESIS 41:17-42:17 MATTHEW 13:24-46 PSALM 18:1-15 PROVERBS 4:1-6	JAN **20**

Application:

1. When Pharaoh elevates Joseph to second in command in Egypt, the patience and trust that Joseph displayed is finally rewarded. Remember, God's rewards might not be given today, but they will be given!
2. Notice the growing guilt that Joseph's brothers display in the readings this week. What guilt torments you?
3. A small amount of faith can develop beyond all expectation. How is God stretching your faith?
4. What is God calling you to give up in order to pursue the Kingdom of Heaven?
5. How has God revealed Himself as your Strength?

GENESIS 42:18-43:34 MATTHEW 13:47-14:12 PSALM 18:16-36 PROVERBS 4:7-10	JAN **21**

Application:

1.   "Surely we are being punished because of our brother." (Genesis 42:21) Guilt is a relentless hunter. Once we are caught in the shadow of guilt, we can only escape it through the blood of Christ. What unconfessed sin do you need to bring to God today?

2.   The parables of Jesus clearly reveal that a judgment is coming. What must you do to be ready for that day?

3.   If you are in tumultuous water or slipping on uncertain sand today, remember that God will rescue you and give you firm footing. Cry out to Him today and ask for His stabilizing Hand to work in your life.

4.   Does your life reflect the pursuit of wisdom? What can you do to grow in wisdom?

GENESIS 44:1-45:28 MATTHEW 14:13-36 PSALM 18:37-50 PROVERBS 4:11-13	JAN **22**

Application:

1. Joseph forgave, in the power of God's mercy. Who is desperately longing for your forgiveness today?

2. A key to Joseph's forgiveness was his trust in the sovereignty of God. Joseph trusted that God was in control. Can you trust Him? Where do you struggle trusting God?

3. Jesus constantly practices the discipline of withdrawal. He retreats from the press of the crowd to spend time with His Father. Schedule some secluded time with your heavenly Father this week.

4. Peter was willing to leave the security of the boat to approach His Master. Do you have the courage to walk to Jesus? What boat is Jesus calling you to leave?

GENESIS 46:1-47:31 MATTHEW 15:1-28 PSALM 19:1-14 PROVERBS 4:14-19	JAN **23**

Application:

1. God is a God of reunions. In this narrative he reunites Joseph with his father. The New Testament speaks of a day of joyous reunion as well. One day Christ will return with those who have died. Who are you longing to see on that day of reunion?

2. Before his death, Jacob demands that Joseph promise to bury him in the Promised Land. This promise points Joseph and the nation of Israel back to God's Promise. How does your life point people to God's promises?

3. The Pharisees were more concerned with the teachings of the elders than with the law. It is a frightful and disturbing position to place tradition above God's Word. Search your own life and find places where you have allowed tradition (the words of man) to have priority above the Bible.

4. Jesus tests the faith of a Gentile woman. She continues to cry out to God and receives a favorable response. Don't lose heart in your petitions. Continue to cry out to God.

5. "May the words of my mouth and the meditation of my heart be pleasing in your sight, O Lord, my Rock and my Redeemer." (Psalm 19:14) Make this your active prayer today. Ask the Holy Spirit to watch your words and thoughts closely, revealing those that are not pleasing to the Father.

GENESIS 48:1-49:33 MATTHEW 15:29-16:12 PSALM 20:1-9 PROVERBS 4:20-27	JAN **24**

Application:

1. The Genesis account is filled with stories of families who "skip" the proper birth order. The firstborn is supposed to receive the blessing but time and time again this does not take place. Remember, that God's plans are not dependent on human factors.

2. Jacob blesses his sons. Fathers and grandfathers, how can you bestow a blessing on your descendants today?

3. Jesus repeatedly says to the disciples, "You of little faith." (Matthew 16:8) How would Jesus describe your faith?

4. Where do you place your trust? Do you trust in your bank account, your country, or your physical strength?

_____

_____

_____

_____

_____

_____

_____

GENESIS 50:1 - EXODUS 2:10 MATTHEW 16:13-17:9 PSALM 21:1-13 PROVERBS 5:1-6	JAN **25**

Application:

1. Joseph's brothers continue to display characteristics of guilt and deceit after their father's death. Interesting how the two constantly travel together. Is guilt producing deceit in your life? Confess and stop the pattern.

2. For the centuries of slavery in Egypt, the people saw Joseph's remains as a reminder that God would provide. What reminds you of your Promised Land?

3. The world offers many opinions of Jesus. What is yours? Ultimately, we must all answer the question that Jesus posed to his disciples. Who do you say that He is?

4. Are you willing to give up your life for Jesus? Not to take a terrorist's bullet and die an immediate death, but rather to die to self each day and give up everything for His sake. What is he calling you to surrender today?

5. At the mount of Transfiguration, Peter tried to build shelters so they could stay on the Holy Mountain. Peter could not, (and neither can we), freeze frame God. We must descend to the valley in order to engage the world! How is God calling you to engage the world?

EXODUS 2:11-3:22	JAN
MATTHEW 17:10-27	
PSALM 22:1-18	**26**
PROVERBS 5:7-14	

Application:

1. Moses committed murder and God used him to lead the nation of Israel to freedom. What past mistakes do you hide behind when God calls you to obedience?

2. When God calls you to a task, do you make excuses or do you make footprints of obedience? What excuses prohibit your obedience?

3. When have you seen a mustard seed of faith move a mountain?

4. Yes, Jesus said that you have to pay your taxes!

5. The selection from Proverbs begs us to ask ourselves, "Is it worth it?" Are the things that command your time, talent, and energy really worth it? Take a look at your calendar and your checkbook and ask that question, "Is it worth it?"

_____

_____

_____

_____

_____

_____

EXODUS 4:1-5:21 MATTHEW 18:1-20 PSALM 22:19-31 PROVERBS 5:15-21	JAN **27**

Application:

1. What is that in your hand? We easily recite the list of things that we cannot do for God. But the better question is what has God placed within us that we can do and must do? What has God given you to use for His Kingdom?

2. Moses begged God for help and he got Aaron. (The same Aaron who later fashioned a golden calf for the people to worship.) Be careful what you ask for!

3. The Israelites rejoiced to know that God had heard their pleas. This reminds us that our "unanswered prayers" have not fallen on deaf ears. Keep lifting your petitions to God.

4. Jesus said, "Woe to the world because of the things that cause people to sin!" (Matthew 18:7). How is media causing you to sin?

5. In Matthew 18, Jesus provides a prescription for dealing with conflict. Write down the name of one individual with whom you need to seek reconciliation. Pray for that person and set a time when you can contact them and follow Jesus' prescription for dealing with conflict.

| EXODUS 5:22-7:25
MATTHEW 18:21-19:12
PSALM 23:1-6
PROVERBS 5:22-23 | JAN
28 |

Application:

1. Moses discovers that leadership and obedience are never popular. How is popular opinion attempting to steer you away from the narrow path of obedience?

2. As you read of the Egyptian plagues, remember that each plague assaulted the authority of an Egyptian deity. God will remove the idols from your life, either by willful submission or by force.

3. The parable of the unmerciful servant reveals a person with spiritual Alzheimer's. They have forgotten the grace they received. How is your spiritual memory? Spend some time thanking God for the mercy you have received and you might find it a little easier to display mercy to others.

4. The shepherd Psalm reminds us that the Lord is our Shepherd. Try praying Psalm 23 to your Shepherd today.

EXODUS 8:1-9:35	JAN
MATTHEW 19:13-30	
PSALM 24:1-10	**29**
PROVERBS 6:1-5	

Application:

1. God struck the nation of Egypt while protecting the land of Goshen, where the Israelites resided. When have you experienced the protection of God? List at least three instances when God protected you and take a moment to share one of them with a co-worker or family member today.

2. How could Pharaoh continue to harden his heart? There is certainly an element of God's Providence; Scripture tells us that God hardened Pharaoh's heart so that He could reveal Himself. However, after seeing all these miracles, how could Pharaoh not repent? What is your excuse for perpetual disobedience?

3. Jesus valued children. It is so important for children to be nurtured and developed both physically and spiritually. How are you nurturing the children God has given you? Are you willing to give of yourself to nurture other children? Is God calling you to open your home to a child in need of a family so that they can receive the physical and spiritual nourishment that all children need?

4. The earth and all within it are the property of God. Praise him for His dominion over all things.

EXODUS 10:1-12:13 MATTHEW 20:1-28 PSALM 25:1-15 PROVERBS 6:6-11	JAN **30**

Application:

1. Pharaoh wavers back and forth between submission and arrogance. The same battle rages within each of us. What must you do today to submit yourself to the Lord and repent of arrogance?

2. The Passover account must be read by Christians with an eye toward the sacrifice of Jesus on the cross. The Passover lamb foreshadows the culmination of God's redemptive plan. Praise God today for His Passover Lamb.

3. That's not fair! The parable of the day laborers Jesus told reminds us that life is rarely fair. It also reminds us that grace is not fair. Thank God for his unfair grace!

4. While some sin in their addiction to work, others sin in their sloth. Which describes you? How would your co-workers describe you?

EXODUS 12:14-13:16 MATTHEW 20:29-21:22 PSALM 25:16-22 PROVERBS 6:12-15	JAN **31**

Application:

1. When the children ask why you commemorate the Passover, tell them! Again, parents we have an incredible, God-given responsibility to nurture our children in their faith. You are never too old to lead your children spiritually! What can you do to facilitate spiritual growth in your children?

2. The Israelite slaves carried the jewelry of the Egyptians as they traveled toward freedom. What an incredible picture of Redemption! Praise God for his Redemption!

3. Jesus embodied compassion. How can you reflect Christ's compassion today?

4. Proverbs warns against deceit and dissension. Both will demolish the church and the witness of the body. Pray that God would cleanse your heart of any deceit or dissension. Also pray that God will protect your church from these destructive elements.

_____

_____

_____

_____

_____

FEBRUARY

| EXODUS 13:17-15:18
MATTHEW 21:23-46
PSALM 26:1-12
PROVERBS 6:16-19 | FEB
1 |

Application:

1. God's direction also provides protection. God did not allow Israel to go the shorter route because he knew they would face battles. Think back on your life and thank God for the times he has taken you the long way to help you avoid pitfalls!

2. At the precipice of our greatest fears we often discover the extent of God's power! God led the Israelites into a trap of despair in order to reveal His power. Remember, that God is in control of your life as well, no matter how close the Egyptians come. What fears are you facing today?

3. In the gospels, Jesus often rebukes the Pharisees specifically and Israel in general for their inability to recognize God's activity among them. I always try to look closely at the warnings directed at the Pharisees in order to guard against repeating the same sins. Where are you missing the activity of God in your life? Ask the Holy Spirit to open your eyes to His work in your lives.

4. Pray over the Proverbs and ask the Holy Spirit to reveal if any of the "detestable" things have crept into your life.

_____

_____

_____

EXODUS 15:19-17:7 **MATTHEW 22:1-33** **PSALM 27:1-6** **PROVERBS 6:20-26**	**FEB** **2**

Application:

1. The Israelites seem to have amnesia. They quickly forget God's gifts and grumble about their circumstances. What are you complaining about today?

2. God provided for the needs of Israel. The provision might not have been fancy, but it met their needs. Thank God for His provision in your life.

3. Are you giving God His portion of your finances as regularly as you give to Caesar? If not, what do you need to do to make giving a part of your life?

4. What fears invade your life? Give them to God.

_____

_____

_____

_____

_____

_____

_____

EXODUS 17:8-19:15 MATTHEW 22:34-23:12 PSALM 27:7-14 PROVERBS 6:27-35	FEB 3

Application:

1. Joshua led the physical attack while Moses led the spiritual attack. Are you diligent in prayer, covering the ground troops with spiritual protection? How can you pray for those on the front lines of spiritual warfare: pastors, missionaries, leaders of non-profit organizations, etc.?

2. Jethro, father-in-law of Moses, is the father of delegation. What tasks should you delegate today?

3. Does your life overflow with love? What can you to foster your love for God? What can you do to foster your love for man?

4. Jesus rebukes the Pharisees for external religious acts. What are you performing in public that you are not practicing in private?

5. How are you playing with the fire of temptation? Don't ignore the warning lights or you will get burned!

EXODUS 19:16-21:21 MATTHEW 23:13-39 PSALM 28:1-9 PROVERBS 7:1-5	FEB **4**

Application:

1. How would you evaluate yourself at keeping the Ten Commandments? God's laws reveal God's character and nature. They also reveal God's expectations for righteousness. The 10 commandments point us toward the Redemption of God in Jesus Christ, the perfect sacrifice for imperfect sinners. Thank God today for His law and His gift!

2. What do the Ten Commandments reveal to you about God's character and his expectations?

3. Jesus delivers a scathing rebuke to the Pharisees. Look closely at each rebuke and ask yourself, "Could Jesus say the same of me?"

4. Are you making a habit of memorizing God's commands? Select one verse of Scripture from your Bible reading and memorize it this week.

_____

_____

_____

_____

_____

EXODUS 21:22–23:13	FEB
MATTHEW 24:1–28	
PSALM 29:1–11	5
PROVERBS 7:6–23	

Application:

1. Notice how God protects the rights of the oppressed: the aliens and orphans (Exodus 22:21-23). How can you imitate God's heart by reaching out to the oppressed?

2. The disciples were enamored with the Temple. Jesus revealed that the Temple would be destroyed. God's plans can never be reduced to buildings! How do your actions and attitudes put more trust in church buildings than in the human structure that is the church?

3. While the "signs of the time" of Christ's return are often debated, one thing is certain Christ will return! If you knew that Christ would return in two weeks, what would you do differently? Go ahead and begin practicing those things now!

4. The reading from Proverbs reveals the subtle temptation of seduction. Make a list of areas where you are tempted. Pray that God will protect your path against such pitfalls

_____

_____

_____

_____

_____

EXODUS 23:14-25:40	FEB
MATTHEW 24:29-51	
PSALM 30:1-12	**6**
PROVERBS 7:24-27	

Application:

1. Are you giving the first fruits of your income to God? If we wait until all the bills are paid, we will never have enough. If we give from the first fruits, we will always have enough!

2. The people send Moses as their spokesperson because they are afraid of God's presence. Do you settle for hearing about God second hand? God gives us the privilege of speaking to Him personally... Take advantage of it! How can you spend time with God this week?

3. Imagine what the glory of God descending on Mount Sinai must have looked like. Spend some time praising God for His glory.

4. Are you being a good steward of what God has given you as you await His return? How can you use your time, talent, and treasure to honor Him?

5. Praise God for the moments that He lifted you from the depths.

_____

_____

_____

_____

EXODUS 26:1-27:21	FEB
MATTHEW 25:1-30	
PSALM 31:1-8	**7**
PROVERBS 8:1-11	

Application:

1. God calls His people to prepare for Him a place of worship. Corporate worship is an important component in the life of a follower of God. How do you prepare yourself for corporate worship?

2. The parable of the virgins reminds us to be prepared for the return of Christ. Does your life display preparedness? What can you do to keep the imminent return of Christ on your consciousness?

3. The parable of the talents reminds us that we must be willing to take risks in order to make gains. The servant who is condemned by the master was content to maintain what he had been given. As a church and as individuals, we can never be satisfied with maintaining. What must you do to overcome the fear of risk taking and seek to advance His Kingdom.

4. When have you discovered that God is your refuge? Thank God for those moments.

5. How can you seek wisdom?

EXODUS 28:1-43 MATTHEW 25:31-26:13 PSALM 31:9-18 PROVERBS 8:12-13	FEB 8

Application:

1. As we read the OT descriptions of the tabernacle and the priesthood, it is important to remember that the New Testament often refers to the followers of Christ with Old Testament imagery. For example, 1 Peter 2:9 refers to believers as a royal priesthood. The priest wore a turban with the message "Holy to the Lord." How does that label fit you? What changes could you make, in the power of the Holy Spirit, to make that label more appropriate?

2. What could you do for "the least of these"?

3. How do you harmonize the need to help the poor expressed in Chapter 25 with the extravagance of the women's worship in Chapter 26?

4. Are you, like the Psalmist, in distress today? Pray this Psalm to God (out loud if you are alone). If you are not distressed, pray this Psalm for someone you know is hurting.

5. Where are you allowing evil to make inroads in your life?

_____

_____

_____

_____

EXODUS 29:1-30:10 MATTHEW 26:14-46 PSALM 31:19-24 PROVERBS 8:14-26	FEB 9

Application:

1. Why did Judas betray Jesus? Scholars have numerous theories. Some assume that Judas was God's pawn. Others think that Judas became frustrated because Jesus would not lead an earthly revolution. Others think that Judas was mad about the use of funds (sounds like a church issue!) The latter options indicate that Jesus wasn't who Judas expected. Do you betray Jesus when your expectations of Him differ from His revelation of Himself?

2. Blood represents purification. Notice the connection between the blood of the Old Testament sacrifice, displayed in Aaron's purification, and the words Jesus used to introduce the Lord's Supper. "This is my blood of the covenant." Thank God for the blood of His Son that purifies you from our sin!

3. Peter made a bold boast that he would not leave Jesus. Do you think that you are incapable of turning from God? Watch out, the arrogant tend to fall first and fall hardest!

4. When faced with the most horrific day of his life, Jesus retreated to the Mount of Olives for prayer. How do you find strength in prayer?

EXODUS 30:11-31:18	FEB
MATTHEW 26:47-68	
PSALM 32:1-11	**10**
PROVERBS 8:27-32	

Application:

1. The instructions for the tabernacle reveal that God wanted that structure to be set apart. How does God reveal His Holiness through the tabernacle?

2. Do you observe a Sabbath, a true day of rest and worship? What changes can you make in your schedule to make this possible?

3. Peter drew his sword to face the mob and once again he is rebuked by Jesus. Sometimes it is difficult to know when to act and when to keep still. Ask God to help you recognize the difference.

4. The record of Jesus' trial reveals great miscarriages of justice and incredible physical torment. Never forget the sacrifice that Christ made so you might receive grace.

5. David records the joy of God's forgiveness in Psalm 32. If your bones are wasting away with guilt, accept the grace God extends. Celebrate his forgiveness today!

_____

_____

_____

_____

_____

| EXODUS 32:1-33:23
MATTHEW 26:69-27:14
PSALM 33:1-11
PROVERBS 8:33-36 | FEB
11 |

Application:

1. Israel became impatient and quickly established a new god to worship. Amazingly, they attributed God's deliverance to this golden calf. Where are you directing the worship God deserves?

2. Remember, Aaron was Moses' reward for arguing with God. Considering Aaron's actions, perhaps you should stop arguing with God and simply obey his instructions.

3. Moses interceded for the people. Even when people are steeped in sin, we should intercede for them. Select a group of people steeped in sin and make a commitment to pray for them consistently.

4. The narrative implies that God was seeking a more intimate relationship with His people, but due to their sin and fear they were unable to meet God as he desired. Ask God to remove your sin and fear that you might be able to experience Him as Moses did.

5. Peter goes from drawing his sword to denying His Lord. Consider instances when you made the same slippery slide? Thank God for his forgiveness.

6. The voice that spoke the world into existence silently accepted the punishment for our sins. Praise God that the voice of creation will also welcome you into eternity through the sacrifice of the Son.

EXODUS 34:1-35:9	FEB
MATTHEW 27:15-31	
PSALM 33:12-22	**12**
PROVERBS 9:1-6	

Application:

1. God reveals that He is gracious and forgiving but will also punish. Thank God for His punishment that drew you to His grace.

2. Moses descended the mountain with an obvious God-glow. How do others see the glow of God in your face?

3. Some of the people who clamored for Christ's execution had shouted His hosannas earlier in the week. How could people change their tune so quickly? How do you?

4. Again, Jesus receives a horrific beating prior to His execution. Jesus endured these things for you. Spend a few moments praising your Savior.

5. The eyes of God are on those who fear Him. We must believe this Truth, even when situations and circumstances scream that we've been forgotten. Ask God to help you to see Him, when you feel forgotten.

EXODUS 35:10-36:38	FEB
MATTHEW 27:32-66	
PSALM 34:1-10	**13**
PROVERBS 9:7-8	

Application:

1. One interesting aspect of the construction of the tabernacle is that God calls for those skilled in construction to participate in the process. The community of God needs all the skills, talents and abilities that He has provided for the Body. How can you use your skills and talents for the Kingdom?

2. "My God, my God, why have you forsaken me?" (Matthew 27:46) In order to identify with sin, Jesus had to experience separation from His Father. Praise God today because Jesus experienced separation in order that we could experience fellowship with the Father.

3. While Pilate and the Jewish leaders seem to play powerful parts in this drama, it is important to remember that their parts were directed by the All-Knowing Author! Ask God to remind you of His activity in the world when things seem out of control.

4. Read Psalm 34 as a testimony of a fellow traveler on the journey. Find courage and confidence in another who has experienced a life of faith.

EXODUS 37:1-38:31	FEB
MATTHEW 28:1-20	
PSALM 34:11-22	**14**
PROVERBS 9:9-10	

Application:

1. The material for the tabernacle was obtained through the sacrifices of the community. Members of the community must always sacrifice to build the body. What can you sacrifice for the good of the community of God?

2. The passage in Matthew provides our foundation and our mission:

   a. The empty tomb is our foundation. It reveals that death is defeated and God is All-Powerful. Pray that you would never forget that your faith is firmly founded in a Grave-Emptying God!

   b. The Great Commission, (Matthew 28:18-20), reveals that resurrection power is released in us so that we can make disciples of our Master! Our faith should produce the fruit of other Christ-followers. What can you do to develop disciples of Christ?

3. God promises to be close to the broken-hearted. How can you provide encouragement to the broken-hearted today?

4. The fear of God leads us to wisdom

_____

_____

_____

_____

EXODUS 39:1-40:38 MARK 1:1-28 PSALM 35:1-16 PROVERBS 9:11-12	FEB **15**

Application:

1. Holiness is a primary theme in the institution of the tabernacle and also later in Temple worship. As an instrument of God, how are you set apart as Holy? Ask God to do His refining work on you as He molds you in Holiness.

2. The Israelites in the desert were completely dependent on God. They moved when He moved. They stopped when He stopped. Pray that God will help you to recognize and practice the same utter dependence on God.

3. Mark retells the story of Christ in action sequences. He repeatedly uses the term immediately to convey a sense of movement. If Jesus never changes (Hebrews 13:8), how can the church of Jesus often be so passive and inactive? How can Jesus use you to stir the church from complacency to activity?

4. As you read Mark's gospel, note the activity of Jesus and the reaction of the crowd or the demons.

5. Mark wants his readers to recognize that Jesus is the Christ, the Son of the Living God. Do you recognize this reality or have you fashioned an inactive, insufficient substitute for Jesus? As you read Mark's gospel, ask God to imprint you with an accurate understanding of Jesus.

LEVITICUS 1:1-3:17	FEB
MARK 1:29-2:12	
PSALM 35:17-28	16
PROVERBS 9:13-18	

Application:

1. When the Israelites left Egypt, they were a rag-tag bunch of former slaves with little understanding of God, His expectations or His plan. They had cried to the God of Abraham, Isaac and Jacob to save them, but beyond the stories of the book of Genesis and their own brief and powerful experience in the Exodus, they had no understanding of God, and no written instructions for living. Leviticus provides those instructions as well as a further, deeper revelation of God. As you read Leviticus, look beyond the letter of the law to discover the Spirit of the Law and find what it reveals about God.

2. Leviticus also reveals that no one can live up to the law in its entirety. Therefore, the book of Leviticus foreshadows the grace of God revealed in Christ. Ask God to help you understand grace more fully as you read the book of Leviticus.

3. Jesus practiced the discipline of time alone with God. How can you follow his example?

The healing of the paralytic reveals that Jesus healed and worked miracles in order to reveal his ability to save people from their sins. The Pharisees balk at this assertion. "You can't do that!" When have you told God what he could and could not do?

59

LEVITICUS 4:1-5:19	FEB
MARK 2:13-3:6	
PSALM 36:1-12	**17**
PROVERBS 10:1-2	

Application:

1. In the rigidness of the law, God provides grace and mercy as well. Notice that a stipulation is made that those who cannot afford a certain sacrifice can bring a lesser sacrifice. What can you do to express God's awareness for the less fortunate!

2. The Pharisees wanted to protect their religion from impurity. This zeal for purity led them to reject Jesus. Ironically, Jesus wasn't "pure" enough for them. In what ways do you protect the purity of your religion at the expense of a relationship with Jesus?

3. "The Sabbath was made for man, not man for the Sabbath." (Mark 2:27) God desires a relationship over ritual. How is your faith focused on ritual? How is your faith focused on relationship with God?

4. How are you enjoying "ill-gotten" treasures? Remember, God doesn't allow the ends to justify the means!

LEVITICUS 6:1-7:27	FEB
MARK 3:7-30	
PSALM 37:1-11	**18**
PROVERBS 10:3-4	

Application:

1. The Levitical command about deceit and cheating are still appropriate. In what areas are you tempted to stretch the truth or cheat others?

2. Some of the dietary regulations that God gave were intended for protection. God commanded them not to eat the fat of animals to save them from disease and ill-health. God desires the best for His people. Ask God to help you abstain from immediate pleasure to experience long-term joy.

3. Jesus called the disciples with a special purpose, "Reach the world with my Gospel!" As Christ's followers today we are under the same mandate. How are you involved in the mission?

4. The family of Jesus did not support His earthly ministry. Perhaps your family ridicules you for your faith in Jesus. Take courage, you can chart a new family legacy in Christ!

5. Some read Psalm 37:4 and assume that God will give them anything that they want. Instead, the words of the Psalmist reveal that God changes our desires to match His desires. Where do you see God actively working to adjust your desires to match His heart?

LEVITICUS 7:28-9:6	FEB
MARK 3:31-4:25	
PSALM 37:12-29	**19**
PROVERBS 10:5	

Application:

1. Moses obeyed the instructions that God provided in Exodus. He consecrated Aaron and the tabernacle as instructed. Where are you having trouble obeying God's instructions?

2. As we read about the consecration of the priest and the tabernacle we must remember that the New Testament refers to followers of Christ as priests. How are you consecrated to the Lord!

3. What is your soil type? What prohibits the Word of God from finding fertile ground in your heart? If you are just reading the Bible in order to mark an item off the to-do list, stop now! God wants to transform your life through the reading of His Word. Let the Word bear fruit in your life!

4. "With the measure you use, it will be measured to you" (Mark 4:24). How we treat others has a direct impact on the way God treats us. Based on that revelation, how do you need to adjust your treatment of others?

5. Proverb 10:5 extols the value of diligent work. Evaluate your own work. When do you show diligence and when do you show laziness?

LEVITICUS 9:7-10:20	FEB
MARK 4:26-5:20	
PSALM 37:30-40	**20**
PROVERBS 10:6-7	

Application:

1. God overwhelms Israel with His presence. How is good overwhelming you?

2. The sons of Aaron were destroyed for worshipping God in a way that disobeyed God's instructions. We must worship God on His terms, not on our own. Identify areas in your worship where you are tempted to worship God on your terms rather than His.

3. "Teacher, don't you care if we drown?" (Mark 4:38) The pleas of the disciples rose over the roar of the sea. When have you asked the question, "Jesus, don't you care if I drown?" Reflect on the ways that Jesus revealed His presence in those times.

4. Everyone knew that the demon-possessed man was hopeless, everyone but Jesus. Who are the hopeless cases in your life? Remember, Jesus relishes the opportunity to restore people to their right minds! How can you extend hope to the hopeless?

5. How does it impact your life to discover that Jesus is your stronghold?

LEVITICUS 11:1-12:8	FEB
MARK 5:21-43	
PSALM 38:1-22	**21**
PROVERBS 10:8-9	

Application:

1. This section of Leviticus again offers dietary and hygiene instructions to aid Israel. This reminds us that God expects Holiness from His people. The New Testament reveals that the expectations of God have not changed! Continue to ask for God's gracious help as you seek to display His holiness.

2. Two desperate figures from two different walks of life come to Jesus for healing. Jesus works in both lives, with no distinction based on income or status. God is always more concerned with the heart! When do you allow stereotyping to hamper your responses to others?

3. Are you desperate for the activity of Jesus in your life? What can you change about your attitudes or actions to reveal your desperation for Christ's activity?

4. The psalmist describes the burden of guilt. If you are struggling with guilt, accept God's forgiveness available through Christ.

5. Proverb 10:8 reminds us of the wisdom of listening. How can you stop the "chatter" long enough to hear the wisdom others speak into your life?

_____

_____

_____

LEVITICUS 13:1-59 MARK 6:1-29 PSALM 39:1-13 PROVERBS 10:10	FEB **22**

Application:

1. God was concerned with both the spiritual and the physical condition of his people. The instructions from Leviticus today focus on hygiene laws that are beneficial to good health. What would God say to you about your health and hygiene today?

2. "And he was amazed by their lack of faith." (Mark 6:6) What is the reaction of Jesus when He observes your faith?

3. The grisly story of John's death reveals the character of two men: Herod and John. John stood for righteousness and courageously faced persecution. Herod's decisions were determined by others and he was not willing to repent of his sin. Where do you see more of John in your character? Where do you see more of Herod in your character?

4. How can you live your life in light of the brevity described in Psalm 39?

LEVITICUS 14:1-57 MARK 6:30-56 PSALM 40:1-10 PROVERBS 10:11-12	FEB **23**

Application:

1. The Levitical laws addressed mildew in the home. While these details may seem minute, it is important to consider the concern that God had for His people. He wanted the best for them in all areas of their lives. He wants the best for you as well!

2. Jesus offers rest to His disciples. He was concerned for their physical and spiritual well being. Is the pace of your life too hectic for proper health? Is Jesus calling you to rest? What changes do you need to make in your schedule?

3. The Psalmist testifies of God's rescue. If you are waiting in a slimy pit caked with mud and mire, don't give up, God will restore you to firm ground.

4. When is your mouth a fountain of life and when does it overwhelm others with violence?

5. The Psalmist cries to the Lord for rescue. What do you need to be rescued from today? Cry out to the Lord and ask for deliverance.

LEVITICUS 15:1-16:28	FEB
MARK 7:1-23	
PSALM 40:11-17	**24**
PROVERBS 10:13-14	

Application:

1. Aaron could not enter the presence of the Lord flippantly. Although we are priests before God, we must take seriously the presence of God. What can you do to display more reverence in your prayers?

2. Jesus rebuked the Pharisees for allowing the traditions of men to overshadow the laws of God. What traditions or practices do you have that are not grounded in God's Word?

3. The Pharisees used their religious rituals as an excuse to ignore the physical needs of their family. When are you tempted to hide behind religion instead of extending a hand of compassion to the hurting?

4. Christ's declaration that all foods were clean lifted some of the prohibitions in the Old Testament that we have read recently. It also reveals that God is more concerned with internal transformation than with external ritual. How do you determine your "cleanliness" or holiness?

5. What are you doing to store up knowledge?

LEVITICUS 16:29-18:30 MARK 7:24-8:10 PSALM 41:1-13 PROVERBS 10:15-16	FEB **25**

Application:

1. The Israelites are commanded to bring sacrifices to a designated, central location. This command was likely intended to maintain the community of the nation. If everyone worshipped on their own, without the influence of community, they would miss the encouragement and accountability of their fellow worshippers. Are you consistent in your involvement with your church family?

2. God specifically instructed His people to set themselves apart from the religious practices of other nations. God is unique and worthy of worship that is unique! How are you tempted to allow your worship of God to take on cultural, worldly trappings?

3. Jesus was willing to physically touch those that He healed. How can you get your hands dirty extending the grace of Christ?

4. The Psalmist reminds us that the Lord blesses those who have regard for the weak. How can you aid the hurting?

LEVITICUS 19:1-20:21	FEB
MARK 8:11-38	
PSALM 42:1-11	**26**
PROVERBS 10:17	

Application:

1. The Old Testament law commanded the people to leave extra gleanings for the less fortunate. How does this philosophy conflict with our typical model of taking all for ourselves?

2. Read carefully through this list of "do nots" in Leviticus. Allow the Spirit to convict you of any areas that need confession and repentance.

3. The disciples thought Jesus was talking about physical yeast but he was making a spiritual analogy. How often do you focus more on the physical world while Jesus is concerned with your spiritual condition?

4. Who do you say that Jesus is? This is the most important question in life!

5. What could you do to improve the way you receive constructive criticism?

_____

_____

_____

_____

_____

LEVITICUS 20:22-22:16	FEB
MARK 9:1-29	
PSALM 43:1-5	**27**
PROVERBS 10:18	

Application:

1. God commanded the Israelites that they could not live by the customs of the land they were about to enter. How are you tempted to live by the customs of this world instead of God's kingdom?

2. Peter wanted to stay on the mountain with Jesus, caught up in the incredible moment of the transfiguration. Like Peter, we must learn to keep hiking in our walk with Christ. If we camp out on one mountain, we might miss the view from the next one or we might miss the ministry opportunity in the valley! Ask God to give you the courage to keep moving forward.

3. "I do believe; help me overcome my unbelief!" (Mark 9:24) Can you relate to the father in the story? Ask God to strengthen your faith and deepen your belief.

4. The Psalmist concludes by saying, "Put your hope in God, for I will yet praise him, my Savior and my God." (Psalm 43:5) In spite of circumstances, the Psalmist continues to praise. Regardless of your trials and tragedies, commit to trust your Father!

5. When are you tempted to use your words to spread slander?

| LEVITICUS 22:17-23:44
MARK 9:30-10:12
PSALM 44:1-8
PROVERBS 10:19 | FEB
28 |

Application:

1. God decreed that the people must not bring maimed sacrifices. Instead, they were to bring their very best. Do you give your best to God? How do you give the best of your time, talent, and treasures?

2. Annually the Israelites celebrated the Day of Atonement, a day of sacrifice for the sins of the nation. As Christians, we celebrate the sacrifice of Christ daily, the eternal atonement for our sins. Spend some time praising God for that sacrifice.

3. Like the disciples, are you more concerned with your position in the Kingdom than with the advancement of the Kingdom? God is not concerned with status; He desires humble commitment to the cause. Ask God to help you live your life for kingdom advancement instead of personal promotion.

4. How do you trust in yourself and your resources instead of the powerful presence of God?

5. When does your tongue bring shame to you and God? Ask God to give you power over your tongue.

WHAT NOW?

MARCH

LEVITICUS 24:1-25:46 MARK 10:13-31 PSALM 44:9-26 PROVERBS 10:20-21	MAR **1**

Application:

1. While we cannot stone to death those who blaspheme God, shouldn't we react with Holy indignation when people speak against God? How do you react when you hear God's name taken in vain? What about when the television spews curses against God?

2. The Year of Jubilee was to be a time of refreshment for the land and a time of restoration for those in slavery. Israel rarely observed this instruction. How are we at providing time for rejuvenation? How can you set free those that you hold in the bondage of anger?

3. Ponder the distinction between child-like faith and childish faith. Which best describes you?

4. The Rich Young Ruler loved his wealth more than Jesus. What supplants Jesus on the throne of your heart?

5. How can you use your words to provide encouragement to others?

_____

_____

_____

_____

_____

LEVITICUS 25:47-27:13	MAR
MARK 10:32-52	
PSALM 45:1-17	2
PROVERBS 10:22	

Application:

1. God's promises to the Israelites often came in conditional statements. In Leviticus, God revealed that He would support Israel when they obeyed and oppose them when they rebelled. Is it possible that the difficulties you are facing can be traced to sin and rebellion in your life? (Remember, at times we face obstacles that are unrelated to our obedience, but when the road gets rocky it is always worth a few moments of self-reflection.)

2. Notice that even in proclaiming potential punishment, God leaves the door to repentance open. Turn back to God and He will accept you.

3. The disciples continue to seek prominence in God's kingdom. Are you guilty of the same? When are you tempted to seek status over servanthood?

4. The blind man at Jericho continued to cry out in desperation to Jesus until Jesus healed Him. Sometimes we fail to invest much energy seeking Christ. What can you do to actively seek the Savior?

LEVITICUS 27:14-NUMBERS 1:54 MARK 11:1-26 PSALM 46:1-11 PROVERBS 10:23	MAR **3**

Application:

1. The priests inspected the donations of the people to judge their quality. When are you giving your best to God and when are you giving him leftovers?

2. The people welcomed Jesus with shouts of Hosanna. Isn't it sad that the same lips that praise Jesus can call for his death in a few short days? How are you tempted to deny Jesus when you leave worship and enter the real world?

3. Jesus drove the money changers out of the Temple. They had perverted worship with capitalistic ambition. How would Jesus react to worship in your church?

4. Relying on the strength of God, we need not worry about quaking mountains or raging seas. The Psalmist reminds us that God's power is greater than any act of nature.

_____

_____

_____

_____

_____

_____

| NUMBERS 2:1-3:51
MARK 11:27-12:17
PSALM 47:1-9
PROVERBS 10:24-25 | MAR
4 |

Application:

1. The Levites were set aside by God for work in the Temple. As believers we have all been set aside by God and called to live as His priests. How can you live as a priest in the world?

2. The parable of Jesus reveals that the Israelites perpetually rejected those sent by God to deliver His message. How are you applying the messages of the messengers that God sends into your life? How could you improve the reception and application of the messages?

3. The Psalmist praises God as King. How can you exalt God as the King of your life? Develop a plan to praise God and live under His authority.

4. If you are facing a storm in your life, remember that you can stand firm in the midst of the storm in God's strength!

_____

_____

_____

_____

_____

_____

| NUMBERS 4:1–5:31
MARK 12:18-37
PSALM 48:1-14
PROVERBS 10:26 | MAR
5 |

Application:

1. The priests packing and assembling the tabernacle paint a picture of teamwork that we should imitate in the church today. What is your role in the body and how are you fulfilling that role?

2. The Sadducees did not believe in the resurrection. Do you? Do you believe that this world is not the end? How does that belief impact your life?

3. How can your actions reflect a fervent love for God?

4. How can your actions reflect love for man?

5. The Psalmist concludes the psalm by praising the eternal nature of God. As you consider the temporal nature of this world, praise God for his eternal existence and dominion.

NUMBERS 6:1-7:89 MARK 12:38-13:13 PSALM 49:1-20 PROVERBS 10:27-28	MAR 6

Application:

1. Aaron and his sons were given a specific blessing to place on the people of Israel. How can we, as God's priests, give this blessing to the people around us?

2. Isn't it interesting that God listed the specific offerings of the people in the book of Numbers, considering that fact that we make such a production of keeping our gifts secret. Although Jesus speaks about giving in secret, perhaps we use the shroud of secrecy to hide from accountability. To whom are you accountable in your giving?

3. The teachers of the law valued the quantity of their prayers more than the quality. How do you evaluate your prayers? What can you do to be more sincere in your prayer life?

4. The widow is applauded by Jesus because she gave all that she had. Most contemporary giving comes from excess. What can you give sacrificially to the cause of Christ?

5. Jesus warns of deception surrounding the last days. The warnings still apply. Don't be deceived by those who make false claims. Test the Scripture and remember, the arrival of Christ is not a puzzle to be solved it is a promise to be received!

| NUMBERS 8:1-9:23
MARK 13:14-37
PSALM 50:1-23
PROVERBS 10:29-30 | MAR

7 |

Application:

1. The Israelites celebrated the Passover, reminding them of God's deliverance. Celebrate Christ, your Passover Lamb today!

2. Like Israel in the wilderness, we should follow God each day, waiting for His presence to lead us. Where is God directing you today?

3. Many attempt to pinpoint the day and the hour that Christ will return. This is comical because Jesus said that even He did not know the time and the day. Christ's warnings about His return encourage us to be vigilant. How can you live with the end in mind?

4. In this psalm, we are reminded that God does not need our sacrifices. He gives us opportunities to sacrifice so that we might worship Him. How does this change your perspective on giving to God?

5. Praise God for the times that His way has provided a refuge for you on the journey.

| NUMBERS 10:1-11:23
MARK 14:1-21
PSALM 51:1-19
PROVERBS 10:31-32 | MAR
8 |

Application:

1. The people spent a long time in the desert receiving the law from God. It is important for us to have a solid foundation of faith. What do you need to do to solidify your foundation?

2. Complaining is contagious. How are you infecting others? How are you being infected by others?

3. Gratitude halts complaining in its tracks. Take some time to thank God for your blessings today.

4. The woman anointed Jesus with an extravagant gesture. How can you be extravagant in your worship? Your giving? Your sacrifice?

5. Psalm 51 offers a model of repentance. Follow that model today to insure that you have a clean slate before God.

| NUMBERS 11:24-13:33 MARK 14:22-52 PSALM 52:1-9 PROVERBS 11:1-3 | MAR 9 |

Application:

1. Moses wished that the Spirit of God would rest on all the people. That is exactly what has happened to all believers in Jesus Christ! Pentecost reminds us that the spirit of God is in His people! How do you see God's Spirit at work in you?

2. Kibbroth Hattavah means graves of craving. We have been taught by culture to indulge our cravings. What cravings might lead you down the path to destruction?

3. What characteristics would God need to change in you so that you might display the humility of Moses?

4. Ten spies reported that the land was full of giants. Two argued that God would still win the victory. With which group do you most readily associate?

5. Take a few moments today to reflect on the beautiful symbolism of the Lord's Supper.

6. Jesus needed prayer support from his disciples but they grew weary. How can you support Christ's Kingdom Work in prayer?

NUMBERS 14:1-15:16 MARK 14:53-72 PSALM 53:1-6 PROVERBS 11:4	MAR **10**

Application:

1. Lack of courage often results in memory loss. At the threshold of the Promised Land Israel longed for the chains of Egypt. In what areas do you long for the chains of sin today? In what ways are you enjoying God's Promises?

2. While God's people can experience certain victory with His strength, they experience certain defeat without His presence. When do you attempt to accomplish tasks in your own strength?

3. Poor choices often lead us into a circular path through the wilderness. When have you taken circular detours due to your disobedience?

4. Peter got it. He declared that Jesus was the Christ. We are never sure that Judas got it, but Peter did. Perhaps that is why Peter's denial hurts us even more than that of Judas. When have you denied Christ in your words or actions? Take comfort in Christ's forgiveness of Peter.

5. In what areas do you trust your wealth to protect you?

_____

_____

_____

_____

| NUMBERS 15:17-16:40
MARK 15:1-47
PSALM 54:1-7
PROVERBS 11:5-6 | MAR
11 |

Application:

1. The Israelites were instructed to carry the word of God in tiny boxes that were attached to their clothing. They lived the Word. Ask God to help us do the same. Establish a plan to memorize Scripture.

2. The rebellion of Korah reminds us of the danger of spiritual rebellion. Leadership struggles always result in casualties. How can you model submission to leaders that God has placed in authority over you?

3. Take a few extra moments to soak in the events of the crucifixion: feel the hammers, see the blood, smell the stench, and hear the cries. Meditate on the sacrifice of your Savior and thank Him for His gift.

4. David writes today's psalm while running from Saul. He feels betrayed and abandoned. If you are facing a similar experience, pray this psalm to God today.

5. What evil desires threaten to trap you?

| NUMBERS 16:41-18:32 MARK 16:1-20 PSALM 55:1-23 PROVERBS 11:7 | MAR 12 |

Application:

1. It is much easier to grumble about leadership than to show support. Make a list of things you can do to show support for your spiritual leaders today.

2. In spite of opposition, Moses continued to intercede for the people. How can you pray for your enemies?

3. It is important to remember that God, who raised His Son from the dead, is still in the stone removal business. No matter how great the obstacle appears, God is able to move it! What obstacles litter your path today?

4. The women left the tomb in fear and trembling. How can you maintain that same type of reverence for the resurrection?

5. The Psalmist reminds us to hand our burdens to the Lord so that He can sustain us. Make a list of your burdens and give them to God today.

_____

_____

_____

_____

_____

NUMBERS 19:1-20:29	MAR
LUKE 1:1-25	
PSALM 56:1-13	**13**
PROVERBS 11:8	

Application:

1. Israel complains that the land of Egypt was better than the wilderness. They forgot that God wanted to take them to the Promised Land, not the wilderness. Are you guilty of complaining about the places that your sin has led you? Repent and quit complaining.

2. Luke's gospel claims the authority of a physician who has done his homework. Luke intends to reveal the accurate story of Jesus Christ. This is not to imply that the other gospels are inaccurate, rather Luke likely wrote to contradict some of the false gospels that were floating around. As you embark on reading the third gospel, ask God to continue opening your eyes to the story of His Son.

3. Zechariah receives this miraculous message in the midst of performing the Temple ritual. The location was not incidental. God was revealing to man that the Temple ritual was to be replaced with a personal relationship. When have you reversed the process and made your faith ritualistic?

4. The Psalmist records a lament to God. Perhaps the lament matches your emotions today. Like the Psalmist, trust in God.

NUMBERS 21:1-22:20 LUKE 1:26-56 PSALM 57:1-11 PROVERBS 11:9-11	MAR **14**

Application:

1. The people grew impatient with God. How often do we find ourselves in this predicament? Ask for God's forgiveness for impatient moments and seek His strength for more patience in the future.

2. Even in punishment and judgment, God provides redemption for Israel. This act of mercy foreshadows the sacrifice of Christ. Praise God for His redemptive nature.

3. "...nothing is impossible with God." (Luke 1:37) This common refrain of Scripture is often misconstrued. We often think that God will do anything that we want Him to do. That is not what the phrase implies. Instead it teaches us that God can and will accomplish his purposes in all situations. How does God want to do the impossible through you to accomplish his plan?

4. Spend some time in prayerful praise today. Use Mary's song and the Psalmist's words of praise as a spark for your own praises.

NUMBERS 22:21-23:30	MAR
LUKE 1:57-80	
PSALM 58:1-11	**15**
PROVERBS 11:12-13	

Application:

1. God used a donkey to steer Balaam from a "reckless path." How is God using circumstances in your life to keep you from making destructive choices?

2. Like Balak, the world will attempt to place words in our mouth. The world will try to make us say false things about God. Ask God to give you the strength and courage to speak Truth.

3. Read Zechariah's prophetic praise song (Luke 1:67-79) closely. It clearly points to salvation in Christ. Join Zechariah and "Praise... the God of Israel, because he has come and has redeemed His people." (Luke 1:68)

4. The Psalmist prays for God's justice to be revealed in those who break God's law. Pray today that God would thwart the plans of those who have no regard for His laws.

5. Do you have a problem with gossip? Think about your conversations, do they tend to turn quickly to people who are not present? Confess this sin and ask for God's grace to change.

NUMBERS 24:1-25:18	MAR
LUKE 2:1-35	**16**
PSALM 59:1-17	
PROVERBS 11:14	

Application:

1. Balaam lost financial gain by speaking the truth about Israel. No matter the cost or potential loss, we must speak God's Truth. Where are you tempted to "shade" the truth with gray in order to make a profit or keep peace?

2. Phinehas took a bold stand against sin. At times, we too are called to take bold actions to resist sin, particularly sin in amongst the Body of Christ. How is God calling you to resist sin in your church family?

3. God used the census of a pagan, earthly ruler to fulfill the prophecy of Christ's birth place. Remember, that while situations may appear bleak on the surface, God is working beyond our sight to bring about His plans and His purpose. What concerns you about the world: economics, politics, terrorism, war, etc.? Ask God to help you recognize His activity in the midst of all the struggles.

4. The shepherds glorified God and praised Him for all they had seen. We should display the enthusiasm of the Shepherds when we go into the world. How can you bear testimony to God's faithfulness?

5. Pray for our nation's leaders that they will seek and accept God's wisdom in the important decisions that are made each day.

NUMBERS 26:1-51	MAR
LUKE 2:36-52	**17**
PSALM 60:1-12	
PROVERBS 11:15	

Application:

1. The genealogies of the Old Testament were important to Israel. They reminded the people of their place in God's nation. Those who have discovered the grace of Christ are a part of Christ's kingdom due to spiritual inheritance! Rejoice that you have a place in God's genealogy.

2. Anna, the prophetess, provides an incredible example of perseverance. How are you persevering in prayer and in faith? Though the wait seems lengthy, God's timing is perfect.

3. Jesus informs His parents that He must be about His Father's business. Perhaps we lose Jesus because we are not seeking Him in places where the Father is at work. Where can you join Jesus in being about the Father's business?

4. Is God always on your side? The Psalmist reminds us that we must make sure that we are on God's side rather than presuming that He is on our side. God doesn't join us, we must join Him!

NUMBERS 26:52-28:15	MAR
LUKE 3:1-22	
PSALM 61:1-8	**18**
PROVERBS 11:16-17	

Application:

1. God honors the request of the daughters of Zelophehad, although women typically had no right to land in that culture. God elevated the status of women and offered protection for minorities in Israel. How can you provide encouragement and support for individuals who face discrimination?

2. Moses initiates the process of a transfer of leadership to Joshua. The transfer of spiritual leadership is always difficult as people typically refuse to accept the new leader because of their respect for the previous leader. Israel accepted the leadership of Joshua and he led them into the Promised Land. How do you accept spiritual leadership?

3. John the Baptist introduced the idea that repentance should be accompanied by fruit. How are you bearing fruit that confirms your repentance?

4. The Psalmist longed to stand on "the rock that is higher than I." (Psalm 61:2) Do you need to stand on that rock today? If you are battered by the world, stand firm on the security of Christ.

5. How do your actions gain respect among your co-workers?

_____

_____

_____

NUMBERS 28:16-29:40	MAR
LUKE 3:23-38	
PSALM 62:1-12	**19**
PROVERBS 11:18-19	

Application:

1. The Israelites were instructed to offer sacrifices to observe specific days that reminded them of God's activity. What special days do you commemorate in your spiritual journey?

2. Luke traces his genealogy of Jesus back to Adam. This is likely because Luke wrote to a Gentile (non-Jewish) audience. This should encourage those of us who are not Jews that the Messiah was intended for us as well! Thank God for breaking the ethnic barriers and extending faith to all nations.

3. How are you depending on wealth, knowledge, gadgets and good works for salvation? Remember, God alone can save through Jesus Christ!

4. Allow God to be your refuge in times of trouble!

| NUMBERS 30:1-31:54
LUKE 4:1-30
PSALM 63:1-11
PROVERBS 11:20-21 | MAR
20 |

Application:

1. Numbers reminds the people of Israel of the significance of an oath before God. How often people make commitments to God that they never keep (or never intend to keep). What must you do to honor your commitments before God?

2. God wins a great victory over Midian. Though the destruction of the Midianites seems brutal by our standards, God is punishing the nation of Midian for enticing Israel to sin. Sin always has consequences! When have you endured painful consequences for your sin?

3. Jesus provides a pattern for resisting the temptation of Satan. Know the Word of God! Do you know Scripture? Do you have it tucked away in your memory so that you can use it against the temptation of Satan? Begin memorizing Scripture today.

4. Too often we are satisfied with the world instead of earnestly seeking God. Do you thirst for God? What could you do to increase your thirst for God?

_____

_____

_____

_____

NUMBERS 32:1-33:39	MAR
LUKE 4:31-5:11	**21**
PSALM 64:1-10	
PROVERBS 11:22	

Application:

1. The Reubenites and the Gadites pledged to do their part in the conquest of the land even though they were to receive land on the other side of the Jordan River. Are you doing your part in the Body of Christ? How are you making your contribution? What more could you do?

2. The travel log of Israel's wandering might seem like dry reading, but each spot on that list represented a place where God revealed Himself to Israel. Each spot represented tangible expressions of Israel's obedience to God. Take a moment and jot down some mile markers on your spiritual journey. Make note of how God has directed you. (It might help you see where God is directing you.)

3. Jesus made time for fellowship with the Father. When can you plan time in your day to spend with God?

4. God calls his followers to fish for men. How are you casting your nets for a spiritual harvest?

5. The Proverb reminds us that beauty is far less important than wisdom! How can you grow in wisdom?

| NUMBERS 33:40-35:34
LUKE 5:12-28
PSALM 65:1-13
PROVERBS 11:23 | MAR
22 |

Application:

1. God commanded Israel to root out the inhabitants of the land. This command was intended to keep Israel free from the hindrance of sin. What inhabitants of the land need to be driven out of your life?

2. The cities of refuge reveal the grace of God for his people. He provides them a safe haven. Do you need to find a safe haven in God today or could God use you to offer a safe haven to someone else?

3. "Friend, your sins are forgiven" (Luke 5:20) Ponder that proclamation. God, through Christ, offers to forgive your sin. Celebrate the freedom of forgiven sin!

4. What is God calling you to leave behind in obedience to Him?

5. The Psalmist writes of forgiveness and blessing. Use the psalm as a guide for your own song of praise to God.

_____

_____

_____

_____

_____

NUMBERS 36:1-DEUTERONOMY 1:46 LUKE 5:29-6:11 PSALM 66:1-20 PROVERBS 11:24-26	MAR **23**

Application:

1. Moses provides a historical review of Israel's wandering. Moses wanted to remind the people of God's faithfulness and inspire the people to be faithful to God. Take a few moments to retrace your spiritual journey.

2. How can you eat with "sinners" and share the Good News?

3. The Pharisees condemned Jesus because they were intent on protecting their religion from humanity. In short, they didn't have much room for man in their religious system. How do your religious habits make room for man?

4. Read aloud Psalm 66 as a song of praise to God.

5. How can you refresh others with your words and deeds?

DEUTERONOMY 2:1-3:29 LUKE 6:12-38 PSALM 67:1-7 PROVERBS 11:27	MAR **24**

Application:

1. Moses reminded the people of Israel of God's protection and provision in the past. Praising God for past provision will typically help us trust Him in the uncertainty of the future. Take a few moments to list events in the past when God protected you or provided for you. Share at least one of those events with someone else today.

2. Jesus dedicated time in prayer before calling the twelve disciples. Do you have an important decision upcoming? Set aside intentional time with God!

3. Pray that God will help you love your enemies. List specifically those with whom you are having difficulties.

4. How are God's blessings in your life leading others to fear Him? What can you do to tell others about God's blessings in your life?

_____

_____

_____

_____

_____

_____

DEUTERONOMY 4:1-49 LUKE 6:39-7:10 PSALM 68:1-18 PROVERBS 11:28	MAR **25**

Application:

1. Moses reminds the people that God's continued favor is contingent on their obedience. Is life assaulting you from all sides? It could be that you have veered away from God's path. Take inventory of your life and ask yourself, have I been faithful to Him?

2. In this recounting of the past, Moses is reminding the people of God's provision and therefore His right to expect obedience to the law. God is the sovereign Lord of history. He retains the right to rearrange your life! Yield yourself to His authority.

3. Do you consistently practice self-reflection? The Pharisees ignored the plank in their own eye while trying to remove sawdust from their neighbor's eye. Take care of your own sin before you seek to engage the sin of others.

4. In what areas of your life are you hesitant to submit to Christ's Lordship?

5. The Psalmist speaks of God's comfort to the oppressed; the fatherless, the widow, the lonely, and the prisoner. What can you do to aid God in his quest to provide for those in need?

_____

_____

_____

DEUTERONOMY 5:1-6:25	MAR
LUKE 7:11-35	
PSALM 68:19-35	**26**
PROVERBS 11:29-31	

Application:

1. Moses repeats the Ten Commandments for Israel as they prepare to take the Promised Land. Take a few moments to review the Ten Commandments again and ask God to reveal the spirit of each.

2. "Do not turn aside to the right or to the left." (Deuteronomy 5:32) What tempts you to veer off course today?

3. This section of Deuteronomy, known as the Shema, reminds parents of their obligation to nurture their children spiritually. What can you do to teach your children and grandchildren the ways of God?

4. Jesus interrupts a funeral procession and rebukes the darkness of death. While the widow's son was resuscitated, God promises that we will be resurrected. Praise God that death is not the end!

5. John the Baptist needed further assurance that Jesus was the Christ. Don't be discouraged when Satan sends doubts your way. Christ is willing to offer hope to those who doubt.

DEUTERONOMY 7:1-8:20 LUKE 7:36-8:3 PSALM 69:1-18 PROVERBS 12:1	MAR **27**

Application:

1. God selected Israel out of His love for Israel, not due to their strength as a nation. God redeemed us through Christ in love, not because He needed us. In what areas are you tempted to think that God needs your assistance?

2. God calls Israel to overcome insurmountable odds. With His strength all things are possible! What is God calling you to overcome?

3. God's discipline is an act of love, not anger. If you sense the rebuke of God today, thank Him and return to Him.

4. The woman with the perfume made an extravagant gesture of devotion. When was the last time that you acted extravagantly toward Jesus? What could you do to display such extravagance?

5. In what areas of your life are you unwilling to accept God's correction? Open you heart and give God complete access today.

DEUTERONOMY 9:1-10:22 **LUKE 8:4-21** **PSALM 69:19-36** **PROVERBS 12:2-3**	**MAR** **28**

Application:

1. Moses promised the people that God would go before them and fight their battles. Where are you running ahead of God's activity?

2. God's commands are given for our benefit not our boredom. Ask God to help you understand His instructions from the proper perspective.

3. What can you change in your life in order to love and serve God with all your heart?

4. How are life's worries choking out your spiritual growth?

5. How well do you listen to God? What can you do to improve your listening skills?

_____

_____

_____

_____

_____

_____

DEUTERONOMY 11:1-12:32 LUKE 8:22-39 PSALM 70:1-5 PROVERBS 12:4	MAR 29

Application:

1. Moses reminded the Israelites that their children had not personally witnessed the miracles of the Exodus. It was the responsibility of the parents to share the rich history of God's activity. Parents, how can you share God's activity with your children?

2. Moses provides a clear picture of God's expectations. Obedience results in blessings, rebellion results in punishment. God's expectations are still the same! How is rebellion causing punishment in your life? How is obedience causing blessings?

3. Jesus displayed dominion over both the natural and the supernatural. How does the dominion of Jesus give you hope today?

4. The first missionary sent by Christ was the man previously possessed by a legion of demons. Jesus told him to share his story. How are you sharing your story with the people you meet?

5. How can you provide value to your spouse?

DEUTERONOMY 13:1-15:23	MAR
LUKE 8:40-9:6	
PSALM 71:1-24	**30**
PROVERBS 12:5-7	

Application:

1. The temptation to worship other gods still exists. What are you doing to resist this temptation?

2. Moses instructs Israel to give a tithe (1/10) of their crops to the Lord. Are you giving a tithe of your income to the Lord? What must you do to begin practicing the discipline of giving?

3. The stories of Jairus and the woman with the issue of blood reveal the desperation of those who approached Jesus. In what ways do you approach Christ with desperation? In what ways do you approach Christ with complacency?

4. Psalm 71 reminds us to take refuge in God. How can you find strength and support from God today?

5. Where do you seek advice? How would you evaluate the advice you receive?

DEUTERONOMY 16:1-17:20 LUKE 9:7-27 PSALM 72:1-20 PROVERBS 12:8-9	MAR **31**

Application:

1. Moses reminded the Israelites to celebrate the Passover. The meal that Jesus celebrated with his disciples prior to the crucifixion was a part of the Passover legacy. Meditate for a moment on the similarities between God's deliverance from Egypt and God's deliverance through Christ!

2. The political ruler of Israel was instructed to study the law on a daily basis so that he could faithfully obey the Lord's commands. Few kings of Israel heeded this command and the results were disastrous for Israel. Pray that your earthly rulers would heed the wisdom of God in their leadership.

3. Who do you say that Jesus is? Does your life support your assertion? If you were placed on trial for being a follower of Christ, what evidence would you provide?

4. Proverb 12:9 warns against living beyond our means. Are you living within the income God has provided or do you consistently spend money on items that will make you look good in the eyes of the world? How can you adjust your spending habits to better reflect God's plans for your life?

APRIL

DEUTERONOMY 18:1-20:20 LUKE 9:28-50 PSALM 73:1-28 PROVERBS 12:10	APR 1

Application:

1. Do you read the horoscope or listen to the "predictions" of psychics? God's word is clear that these mediums open the path for pagan influences in our lives.

2. The strength of Israel's army resided in God. Do you trust in God's strength or your strength? How can you resist the temptation to trust in your pocketbook, retirement, 401K, friends, technology, or family?

3. Take a few moments to imagine the scene on the Mount of Transfiguration. When we think of heaven, we often think of the images described in Scripture and popularized in our hymns: pearly gates, streets of gold, etc. However, the most incredible part of heaven is not the be-jeweled decorations but the presence of God's glory!

4. Like the disciples we, as followers of Christ, must constantly battle the selfish arrogance that seeks to dominate our existence. When are you tempted to trust in your own ability?

5. Don't fall into the trap of envying the arrogant. Make a list of your heroes, those you model your life after. Make sure that your models are worthy of imitation.

DEUTERONOMY 21:1-22:30	APR
LUKE 9:51-10:12	
PSALM 74:1-23	2
PROVERBS 12:11	

Application:

1. Deuteronomy mixes instructions on safety, purity, and social graces. God cares for His people in every component of their lives. No part of your life is separated from God's influence. What parts of your life do you tend to compartmentalize and separate from God's influence?

2. James and John, appropriately nicknamed the Sons of Thunder, wanted to call down fire on those that rejected Jesus. The rebuke of Jesus reveals that rejecting Jesus is punishment enough. Who would you like to see get their rightful punishment? Remember, judgment is God's job!

3. Which of the excuses that Jesus encountered most resembles the excuses you typically offer?

4. The harvest is plentiful. Are you willing to be a worker for the harvest? What can you do to share the Good News of Christ?

5. There is a time for dreaming and a time for action. God rewards those who couple dreams and action. How can you place your hand to the plow today and accomplish some of the dreams God has placed in your heart?

| DEUTERONOMY 23:1-25:19
LUKE 10:13-37
PSALM 75:1-10
PROVERBS 12:12-14 | APR
3 |

Application:

1. God commands the Israelites to look after the "outcasts" of society. He makes accommodations for the poor, the widows, the aliens, and the hired workers. What causes you to ignore the "least of these?"

2. Make a list of events in the gospel accounts that confirm that Jesus is the Christ.

3. Who is your neighbor? What can you do to be a better neighbor?

4. What are you thankful for today? Take a few moments to make a Thanksgiving list.

_____

_____

_____

_____

_____

_____

_____

DEUTERONOMY 26:1-27:26 LUKE 10:38-11:13 PSALM 76:1-12 PROVERBS 12:15-17	APR 4

Application:

1. The story of the Exodus is repeated often in the Old Testament. While it might seem repetitive to us, we must remember that this miraculous event was their story of God's intervention and deliverance. Similarly, we must never tire of the story of Christ's crucifixion and resurrection!

2. Read over the list of curses provided by Moses. Ask the Holy Spirit to reveal any places in your life that need midcourse correction.

3. I've heard people justify their actions by saying that they are just a "Martha". The problem with that justification is that Jesus rebuked Martha! That would be like justifying our attitudes by saying, "I'm just a Pharisee!" Meditate on how you can practice an attitude like Mary.

4. Persistence in prayer is difficult. Have you given up on any prayer concerns because they took too long? Make a commitment to persevere in prayer in those requests.

5. Have you been insulted recently? Ask God to help you overlook the insults of others. Remember, Jesus instructs us to turn the other cheek.

DEUTERONOMY 28:1-68 LUKE 11:14-36 PSALM 77:1-20 PROVERBS 12:18	APR 5

Application:

1. Today's reading from Deuteronomy reminds the Israelites that the blessings of God are contingent on the obedience of God's people. It was not enough for Israel to rely on their past faithfulness, God expected them to continue to trust Him. How are you living on past-tense faith, relying on past obedience and ignoring present instructions?

2. Jesus overcame the strongman (Satan) when he conquered the grave. Praise God today because you can live in the power of the resurrection!

3. When the Holy Spirit removes sinful habits from our lives, we must strive to replace those habits with positive fruit (the Fruit of the Spirit), because if we simply remove the bad, we will likely only fill the void with other sinful habits. What fruit is God seeking to cultivate in your life"

4. We have heard of reckless driving, but the writer of Proverbs introduces a new concept, reckless speaking. When are you guilty of reckless speech that wounds the people around you? Ask God to help you control your tongue.

DEUTERONOMY 29:1-30:20	APR
LUKE 11:37-12:7	
PSALM 78:1-31	**6**
PROVERBS 12:19-20	

Application:

1. The clothes of the Israelites did not wear out on their 40 year odyssey in the wilderness. It is encouraging to know that God cares for the smallest details of our lives, even when we are in exile! Make a list of the small details that God has taken care of in your life this week.

2. "I will be safe, even though I persist in going my own way." (Deut 29:19) It is easy to live by that erroneous assumption. It is the chief form of calloused indifference that continues in sin saying, "Jesus will forgive whatever sins I commit!" In what ways have you been taking advantage of God's grace?

3. God promises grace to His people, even when they rebel against Him. Grace and mercy are not limited to the New Testament. Ask God to help you see his grace in the pages of the Old Testament.

4. Jesus pronounces a stinging list of woes on the Pharisees. Read each one and ask the Holy Spirit to reveal the places in your life where you resemble the Pharisees more than Jesus.

5. In what areas of your life do you fear earthly things? In what areas of your life do you fear God, who alone controls your eternal destiny?

DEUTERONOMY 31:1-32:27 LUKE 12:8-34 PSALM 78:32-55 PROVERBS 12:21-23	APR 7

Application:

1. It is easier to follow a human being than to trust in an invisible God. Perhaps that might have played a part in God's decision to prohibit Moses from leading Israel into the land of Promise. The people needed to recognize that God, not Moses, had provided the Promised Land. Which human leaders are you tempted to trust more than God?

2. Sharing our faith in Christ can be uncomfortable at times, but Jesus reminds us that if we are ashamed of Him on earth, He will be ashamed of us in heaven. Ask God to grant you the courage to share His story with confidence.

3. When are you tempted to measure your success by material possessions? God works on a different economy. Ask Him to reveal His assessment of your accomplishments.

4. If you struggle with worry, remember worry is not an excusable character flaw. Jesus commands us not to worry. Make a list of your biggest worries. Then, commit each one to God in prayer.

5. Again, Jesus instructs his followers to sell their possessions and give to the poor. What could you give up to help someone in need?

DEUTERONOMY 32:28-52 LUKE 12:35-59 PSALM 78:56-64 PROVERBS 12:24	APR **8**

Application:

1. The song of Moses reminds Israel and us that any god other than Jehovah is insufficient. Make a list of idols that you are tempted to worship. Beside each idol, note how the idol does not deserve your worship.

2. Are you ready for the return of Christ? Preparedness cannot be checked off a list once and marked complete forever. Preparedness occurs on a daily basis, moment by moment seeking to honor God with our lives. What can you do to increase your preparedness?

3. Although Jesus is the Prince of Peace, His Peaceful reign will only ensue after conflict. While we must treat people with respect and love, we must not compromise Truth for peace in our conversations. Identify instances when you are tempted to tell people what they want to hear, instead of telling them what they need to hear.

4. The Proverb reflects the reality of the familiar axiom, "Idle hands are the devil's workshop." When does lack of activity tempt you to sin? Develop strategies to avoid those situations.

DEUTERONOMY 33:1-29 LUKE 13:1-21 PSALM 78:65-72 PROVERBS 12:25	APR 9

Application:

1. Read the words of Moses as a final speech of blessing by an elderly leader. Moses had guided this rag-tag bunch of former slaves for 40 years. Remember, on many occasions the only thing that saved Israel from God's wrath was the tender, humble intercession of Moses. Note the love of Moses for the people as well as the love of Moses for God. If you are a leader, ask God to instill within you this type of love for your people. If you are not a leader, ask God to bless you with humble leaders who display this sort of character and concern. (The Psalmist points out that David also displayed this type of shepherd-like concern for Israel.)

2. Jesus is fanatic about fruit. He desires, expects, and longs for fruit in His followers. Fruit (a changed life) is not optional. How are you bearing fruit? What adjustments could you make to improve fruit production?

3. The parables that Jesus relays about the Kingdom of God reveal that God's kingdom begins small but permeates through the world. We are a part of the Kingdom advancement team. What are you doing to spread the Kingdom of Christ?

4. Words have the incredible power to tear down or build up. Who can you build up with your words today?

DEUTERONOMY 34:1-JOSHUA 2:24 LUKE 13:22-14:6 PSALM 79:1-13 PROVERBS 12:26	APR **10**

Application:

1. The grave of Moses remained a mystery, perhaps because the people would have been tempted to erect a shrine to their leader. Again, we must constantly guard against the temptation to worship God's leaders in place of God.

2. "Be strong and courageous." (Joshua 1) This phrase is a constant refrain in the early chapter of Joshua's leadership. Imagine Joshua replacing Moses. He had big shoes to fill! The reminder to be strong and courageous must have helped the new leader. If God is calling you to a new position of service, perhaps you need to apply those words today as well.

3. This time the report of the spies was one of courage and confidence. We must face the obstacles that God places in our path with confidence in His power! What obstacle is God empowering you to overcome?

4. God's salvation is not obtained through works, but believers should work because they've received God's grace. How are you striving in your salvation, working out the gift that God has placed within you?

5. The actions of the Pharisees consistently reveal that their religious system was more important than the people for whom the system was developed. How have you allowed religion to overshadow your compassion for man?

JOSHUA 3:1-4:24 LUKE 14:7-35 PSALM 80:1-19 PROVERBS 12:27-28	APR **11**

Application:

1. Crossing the Jordan parallels the Crossing of the Red Sea. God wanted the people to know that He was still in control in spite of the death of Moses. What situation are you facing where God is trying to remind you of His control?

2. God instructed Israel to build a monument to remind the people of their entrance into the land of Promise. It is important to mark the milestones of your journey with God. Take a moment to reflect on the monumental moments on your faith-journey.

3. Rather than seeking reciprocation, we should reach out to those who cannot return the favor. Who could you help or encourage that could do little in return?

4. Jesus encourages followers to count the cost of followship. I wonder if the contemporary church has overlooked the value of counting the cost in our efforts to share the Good News. We focus on the eternal benefits (heaven) but we often hide the earthly sacrifice (discipleship). This deceptive presentation disregards Christ's command. If you have accepted Christ as your Savior, take a few moments to contemplate the necessity of making Him your Lord.

5. The Psalmist refers to God as the "Shepherd of Israel" (Psalm 80:1) How do you know that God is your shepherd?

JOSHUA 5:1-7:15	APR
LUKE 15:1-32	
PSALM 81:1-16	**12**
PROVERBS 13:1	

Application:

1. The nations of Canaan melted in fear at the arrival of the Israelites. If we are on the Lord's side, we have nothing to fear from our enemies! Which enemies tempt you to fear? Commit those individuals and circumstances to the Lord.

2. The Lord is not on our side, we must align ourselves with Him to make sure we are on His side. How does your life reflect that you are on the Lord's side?

3. Which strongholds in your life do you need God to destroy? Make a list below.

4. Are you, like Achan, harboring sin? Ask the Holy Spirit to reveal areas in your life where you need to seek God's forgiveness and reveal the clean slate that He offers.

5. The "Lost" parables remind of God's zeal for those who are separated from Him. Meditate on God's zeal for the "lost." Thank God for zealously seeking you and ask Him to instill within you the same passion for the "lost."

JOSHUA 7:16-9:2	APR
LUKE 16:1-18	
PSALM 82:1-8	**13**
PROVERBS 13:2-3	

Application:

1. While the punishment of Achan might seem cruel and unusual, it sends a message about God's zealous passion for Holiness. This was a crucial juncture in the nation's history and God wanted the people to recognize His zeal for Holiness. In what areas are you tempted to allow expediency or selfishness to infringe on God's Holiness?

2. If you are failing at something, take inventory of your life and see if pockets of sin are prohibiting you from accomplishing the task.

3. If you long for a "bigger" ministry opportunity, ask yourself, "Am I being faithful with what God has given me?" How can you serve more effectively in your current position?

4. Look honestly at your life and your checkbook. Ask yourself, "Do I serve God or money?"

5. Do you need to place a sentry over your lips? Ask God to guard your tongue!

_____

_____

_____

_____

JOSHUA 9:3-10:43 LUKE 16:19-17:10 PSALM 83:1-18 PROVERBS 13:4	APR **14**

Application:

1. Do you inquire of the Lord in all things? When are your tempted to trust your own instincts?
2. When have you gone against the Lord's plans? How did the results differ when you obeyed God's instructions?
3. The parable of Lazarus and the Rich man reminds us that we should live for eternal rather than temporary fulfillment! How are you guilty of seeking temporary fulfillment?
4. What do you do that could lead others to sin?
5. Make a list of the people that you need to forgive.
6. Pray the prayer of the disciples, "Increase our faith!"

JOSHUA 11:1-12:24 LUKE 17:11-37 PSALM 84:1-12 PROVERBS 13:5-6	APR **15**

Application:

1. The conquest of the Promised Land was bloody and gruesome. However, the people of the land had sinned by rejecting God. People often speak of "innocent" people groups that do not deserve God's judgment. Is anyone innocent before God?
2. Thank God for the blessings He gives.
3. "The kingdom of God is within you." (Luke 17:21) That statement is radical and revolutionary! How is the Kingdom of God being lived out in your life today?
4. The Psalmist yearns for God. How do your actions display a yearning for God?
5. Take a moment to thank God for the protection He has provided you when you were willing to obey Him. Protection from disease, harm, disappointment, tragedy, etc.

_____

_____

_____

_____

_____

JOSHUA 13:1-14:15	APR
LUKE 18:1-17	
PSALM 85:1-13	16
PROVERBS 13:7-8	

Application:

1. It is somewhat surprising to hear that Joshua is getting old. While it seems Joshua has only recently come to lead Israel, he has been active for a long time as an assistant to Moses. It changes our perspective to consider that Joshua led the attack on the Promised Land at a ripe old age. What type of Kingdom Work have you convinced yourself that you are too old to accomplish? Remember, we never retire from obedience to God!

2. Caleb requests that Joshua give him the land filled with giants. At 80 years old, Caleb's faith and confidence in God had not dimmed any in the past 40 years. He still believed that God would win the victory. What steps can you take to insure that you persevere in faith and continue to trust God?

3. When have you witnessed the positive impact of persistent prayer? Share that example with someone today.

4. Do you ever elevate your own spiritual status by looking down on the faults and sins of others? Remember, our standard is not the sinner on our left; our standard is the Savior above!

5. The Psalmist speaks of God's restoration of Israel. Who do you know that needs God's restoration? Ask God to speak to them and volunteer to be the messenger.

JOSHUA 15:1-63	APR
LUKE 18:18-43	
PSALM 86:1-17	**17**
PROVERBS 13:9-10	

Application:

1. While the description of the distribution of the land might appear tedious, remember that this was the fulfillment of God's promise to Israel. We can always celebrate the fulfillment of God's promises because they remind us that all of God's promises are true! Celebrate one of God's fulfilled promises in your life today. Look for an opportunity to relay that story to someone else.

2. The story of the rich ruler emphasizes our dependency on God for salvation. We cannot earn it! How do you foster a dependent attitude towards God?

3. The blind man pursued Jesus with reckless cultural abandon. Would anyone accuse you of reckless abandon for Jesus?

4. Join the Psalmist in praying for an undivided heart.

5. Pride leads to conflict, wisdom leads to collaboration. Do you often find yourself in conflict with others? How can you temper your pride?

JOSHUA 16:1-18:28	APR
LUKE 19:1-27	
PSALM 87:1-7	**18**
PROVERBS 13:11	

Application:

1. The people of Joseph requested more territory from Joshua. The response from Joshua was, "Go and take more territory from the inhabitants of the land." At times we ask God to expand the kingdom through us and His reply is, "Go take it!" How does God want to use you to expand His kingdom?

2. The story of Zacchaeus is often relegated to the children's department, but it reminds adults of the grace of God and the extravagant response of the forgiven sinner. What is your daily response to God's extravagant grace?

3. Jesus came into this world to seek and to save the lost. How can you actively seek the lost?

4. The parable of the minas indicates that we must be willing to trust God enough to take risks. The third servant is not commended for maintaining the status quo. Instead, he is rebuked for failing to increase the investment he received. How is God calling you to invest the resources He has given you?

5. Don't fall for get-rich-quick schemes. It is easy to find advertisements that offer "immediate" financial rewards. Most of them represent "dishonest money." How can you avoid this trap?

| JOSHUA 19:1-20:9 LUKE 19:28-48 PSALM 88:1-18 PROVERBS 13:12-14 | APR 19 |

Application:

1. The provision for cities of refuge in the Promised Land reveals God's desire to protect His people. God provided a means of mercy and justice for those who accidently took a life. How do you extend God's mercy and justice?

2. "If they keep quiet, the stones will cry out." (Luke 19:40) Are the rocks around you crying out to cover your lack of heart-felt worship? Choose your favorite hymn or chorus and spend time praising God today. Even better, write your own song of praise to the Messiah.

3. Jesus displayed holy anger when he cleared the Temple. What causes holy, righteous anger to well up in you? When is your anger sinful and selfish?

4. If your current situation amplifies the silence of God in your life, pray Psalm 88 as your own prayer to the Lord.

5. Are you open to the instruction and wisdom from those around you? How do you handle spiritual discipline?

JOSHUA 21:1-22:20	APR
LUKE 20:1-26	
PSALM 89:1-13	**20**
PROVERBS 13:15-16	

Application:

1. Joshua 21:43-45 recounts the relief of Israel at the fulfillment of God's promise. "The LORD gave them rest on every side." (Joshua 21:44) List five promises that God has fulfilled and praise Him for each one.

2. When a questionable altar is built by the Reubenites, Gadites and half-tribe of Manasseh, the rest of Israel rushes to the defense of righteousness. How do you react when you see "Christians" engaged in questionable behavior? Ask God to give you the courage to confront and, if necessary, rebuke.

3. The parable of the tenants reveals that the nation of Israel had rejected God's prophets and would soon reject God's son. A legacy of rebellion develops much easier than a legacy of faith. What are you doing to establish a legacy of faith in your family?

4. "I will sing of the LORD's great love forever;" (Psalm 89:1). Have you ever pondered the fact that we will worship God for all eternity? Meditate on the majesty and wonder of worship in heaven.

JOSHUA 22:21-23:16	APR
LUKE 20:27-47	
PSALM 89:14-37	**21**
PROVERBS 13:17-19	

Application:

1. It is not uncommon for conflict to develop among the people of God. Sadly, the people of God rarely use the patience and mercy of God to resolve disputes. The example of the altar built by the Reubenites, Gadites and the half-tribe of Manasseh is informative. The other tribes questioned them on the altar, but then allowed room for explanation. They were ready to go to war if necessary, but they were also willing to listen before they charged into battle. We should learn from this example. Ask God to give you wisdom and discernment when you have conflicts with other believers.

2. The Sadducees were obviously trying to trick Jesus. They didn't even believe in the resurrection! How do you allow "deep theological questions" to derail your faith and obedience? While we should ponder the ways of God, we must remember that His ways are not our ways, and that the primary purpose of God's Word is life transformation!

3. Make a list of the things that you do to impress the people around you. Now make another list of the things that you do to impress God.

4. God is our glory, strength, shield, God and Savior. Praise God with those titles today as you reflect on how He represents those characteristics in your life.

JOSHUA 24:1-33 LUKE 21:1-28 PSALM 89:38-52 PROVERBS 13:20-23	APR **22**

Application:

1. Joshua's farewell speech resembles the parting words of Moses. Both leaders plead with the people to honor God with their lives. What have you done this week to honor God?

2. Does your household serve the Lord? What are you doing to make that happen?

3. Joshua's stone was a constant reminder of the covenant. What reminds you of your covenant with God?

4. The culmination of redemption approaches with the return of Christ. How do you envision the return of Christ? Does it provoke images of horror or images of joy?

5. The psalmist shifts from "How long, O LORD? Will you hide yourself," (Psalm 89:46) to "Praise be to the LORD forever." (Psalm 89:52) Do you occasionally find yourself flipping back and forth as well? Does it encourage you to recognize that the Psalmist also dealt with doubts and uncertainties?

_____

_____

_____

_____

JUDGES 1:1-2:9 LUKE 21:29-22:13 PSALM 90:1-91:16 PROVERBS 13:24-25	APR **23**

Application:

1. Caleb provides an example of boldness as he drives out giants and provides for his family. How can you imitate Caleb's boldness today?

2. The book of Judges begins with a list of Israel's victories, but if you look closely the list is lined with some incomplete grades. They failed to drive out several people groups. Israel didn't finish the job and their incompletes come back to haunt them. What traps are lingering in your list of victories?

3. Like the warnings of Joshua and Moses in the Old Testament, Jesus offers a warning against dissipation, drunkenness and the anxieties of life. What is weighing down your heart and prohibiting you from walking with Christ?

4. Note that Psalm 90 is attributed to Moses. Think of the wilderness journey as you read this Psalm.

5. How can you give (and receive) discipline appropriately?

_____

_____

_____

_____

JUDGES 2:10-3:31 LUKE 22:14-34 PSALM 92:1-93:5 PROVERBS 14:1-2	APR **24**

Application:

1. While we would expect the miraculous provision of God to sustain His children for many generations, they quickly forget about God. What legacy are you leaving for your family? What will help them honor God in future generations?

2. Even in periods of rebellion, God reveals His mercy on Israel by sending judges to win victories and draw Israel back to their God. Thank God for the mercy He has shown you in the midst of rebellion.

3. Take a few moments today to reflect on the sacrifice of Jesus. Perhaps you can take a few moments to observe the Lord's Supper on your own.

4. Peter was ready to follow Jesus to death. But was Peter ready to follow Jesus in life? Why is it sometimes more difficult to live for Christ than to die for Him?

5. Do you have a tendency to embellish facts and mislead others? Repent of your devious ways and seek forgiveness from the God of Truth.

JUDGES 4:1-5:31 LUKE 22:35-53 PSALM 94:1-23 PROVERBS 14:3-4	APR **25**

Application:

1. How easily Israel bounces from victory to despair. Do you find yourself experiencing victories and setbacks almost simultaneously? Ask God to help you find a more consistent rhythm of faith.

2. The song of Deborah seems to praise righteous leaders who are willing to live for the Kingdom of God. If you are a leader, how can you influence others for the Kingdom? If you are not a leader, how can you pray for your spiritual leaders today?

3. Jesus prayed with earnest zeal in the garden of Gethsemane. Drops of blood poured from His body. Christ's emotional intensity reveals that we can approach God honestly. What issues and emotions do you need to honestly bring before God?

4. We, like Peter, are willing to fight for Jesus. While there are times to fight, there are also times to lay down our swords. Pray that God would help you differentiate between the two.

5. Do your words bring you punishment or protection? If your answer is punishment, how can you adjust your words to make a change?

| JUDGES 6:1-40
LUKE 22:54-23:12
PSALM 95:1-96:13
PROVERBS 14:5-6 | APR
26 |

Application:

1. God saw Gideon as a mighty warrior although Gideon's present circumstances screamed the opposite. What does God see in you? If God is calling you to a task that seems out of character, remember God knows you better than you know yourself.

2. Before Gideon could conquer the Midianites, God wanted Gideon to remove the pagan altars from his life. What idols are hindering your ability to follow Jesus?

3. Although God had already spoken, Gideon laid out a fleece so that God would prove His presence. When have you laid out a fleece for God? Was your fleece an indication of faith or fear?

4. Peter's denial of Jesus confronts us because we often deny our Savior by our words and actions. List moments this past week when you have betrayed God with your words or actions then ask God to forgive you of your betrayal.

5. Herod wanted Jesus to perform miracles like a circus sideshow. Is your relationship with Jesus still hovering in the immature realm of miracle-seeking or are you walking in the confidence of faithful-living?

6. Ask God to help you display discernment in your daily choices.

JUDGES 7:1-8:17 LUKE 23:13-43 PSALM 97:1-98:9 PROVERBS 14:7-8	APR **27**

Application:

1. Gideon commanded the incredible shrinking army! When have you questioned God's distribution of resources, people resources or financial resources? Sometimes God thins the army so that His power can be revealed!

2. God crushed the Midianites. What ominous obstacle do you need to commit to God today? He is able to overcome the most formidable foes!

3. "Father, forgive them, for they do not know what they are doing." (Luke 23:34) As a follower of Jesus, how can you practice this type of forgiveness?

4. The thief on the cross reveals that it is never too late for an individual to find Jesus! If you have given up on someone, pray that God would miraculously make Himself known.

5. Shout for joy to the Lord. Go ahead, take a walk, get outside and shout a word of praise to the Lord!

JUDGES 8:18-9:21 LUKE 23:44-24:12 PSALM 99:1-9 PROVERBS 14:9-10	APR **28**

Application:

1. Gideon refused the role of king but he took for himself many of the spoils of a king: a harem, an ephod, etc. Gideon's actions, particularly with the ephod, proved a stumbling block for Israel. God is the only King! When are you tempted to establish yourself on the throne of your life?

2. "Into your hands I commit my Spirit." (Luke 23:46) The mission is complete, the job is finished! Jesus completed the mission of seeking and saving the lost. Thank God that your salvation is secured in the completed work of Christ.

3. Seeing only the death of Jesus, the centurion could bear testimony to the righteousness of Christ. Having read the entire gospel (three times now!), what is your testimony of Christ's righteousness?

4. The disciples initially doubted the resurrection report of the women. How does your life reflect your belief in the resurrection?

5. Fools leave animosity unresolved but the wise foster good will. Who do you need to approach and seek their forgiveness for sins you have committed?

JUDGES 9:22-10:18 LUKE 24:13-53 PSALM 100:1-5 PROVERBS 14:11-12	APR **29**

Application:

1. The story of Abimelech reveals that God punishes sin. While some might seem to avoid judgment now, God will dispense justice! Commit to God the areas where you struggle because sin seems to go unpunished. Ask Him to help you trust Him with those issues.

2. The stories of Tola and Jair are brief. Essentially, God worked through them to save Israel. What is God doing through you?

3. The hearts of the Emmaus bound travelers burned within them when they recognized Jesus. How does your heart burn with the power of the resurrection?

4. Jesus tells the disciples that they are His witnesses. What sort of witness for the resurrected Jesus have you been this week?

5. We often navigate life with our own internal GPS. The Proverb warns that our GPS might seem right to us, but unless it is calibrated with the Holy Spirit, we will likely veer far off God's course! Ask the Holy Spirit to calibrate your GPS.

JUDGES 11:1-12:15	APR
JOHN 1:1-28	
PSALM 101:1-8	**30**
PROVERBS 14:13-14	

Application:

1. Jephthah overcame a questionable birth, (son of a prostitute), to lead Israel. Remember, God is more concerned with where you are headed than with where you have been. What issues from your past have you allowed to hinder your present progress in Christ?

2. When have you made an unnecessary and ill-advised promise to God?

3. Jesus existed with God before the beginning of time. There has never been a day that Jesus didn't exist, nor will there be a day he doesn't exist. How do these realities impact your life?

4. "The Word became flesh and made his dwelling among us." (John 1:14) Spend some time today praising God that He sent His Son into our world to walk a mile in our shoes and reveal the only path to a relationship with Him.

5. The Psalmist commits to lead a blameless life. Make a similar commitment to God and ask for the power of the Holy Spirit to empower you in that commitment.

WHAT NOW?

MAY

JUDGES 13:1-14:20 JOHN 1:29-51 PSALM 102:1-28 PROVERBS 14:15-16	MAY **1**

Application:

1. Manoah is not the first parent to ask God for wisdom on raising their child. Parents, ask God for wisdom today. Remember, even adult children need the influence of a Godly parent.

2. Impatience and anger dominate Samson's life. Do these two hostile agents hold you hostage as well? Confess your impatience and anger and ask for God's forgiveness and transformation.

3. John models humility in His relationship with Jesus. How can you model humility in your relationship with Jesus?

4. Where would the church be without Peter? Without the witness of Andrew, Peter would never have discovered Jesus. Is there a Peter waiting to hear about Jesus from you?

5. In the midst of turmoil, the Psalmist seeks security in God. Perhaps you need to follow that example today.

_____

_____

_____

_____

_____

JUDGES 15:1-16:31 JOHN 2:1-25 PSALM 103:1-22 PROVERBS 14:17-19	MAY 2

Application:

1. In addition to impatience and anger, Samson also displays a weakness for women. How many men (and women) have been crippled by their inability to control their sexual desires? Are you bound by sexual sin? Repent, and seek God's help!

2. While Samson destroys many Philistines with his final act, we can only imagine what Samson could have done without his tragic flaws. What tragic flaws are hindering your effectiveness in the Kingdom of God?

3. Compare the righteous indignation of Jesus clearing the Temple to the selfish anger of Samson. Which do you resemble most? How can you transform your selfish anger to righteous indignation?

4. God casts our sin as far as the east is from the west. What confessed sin is the accuser bringing back to your mind today? Remember, confessed sin that is brought back to our mind, is brought by Satan not God.

5. Appropriately, considering the narrative on Samson, the Proverb reminds us of the folly of quick-tempered actions. Make a list of the moments you are most likely to lose your temper. Ask God to help you in each of those moments.

| JUDGES 17:1-18:31
JOHN 3:1-21
PSALM 104:1-23
PROVERBS 14:20-21 | MAY
3 |

Application:

1. Micah's mother helps direct him toward idolatry. Parents, what idols are you encouraging your children to follow? How can you steer them away from idols?

2. Micah created his own system of worship (ephod, priest, shrine, etc.). How does your pattern of worship reflect the Truth revealed in God's Word? How is your worship man made?

3. Have you ever been born again? Take a few moments to reflect on your second birth. Thank God for the gift of life.

4. Can you quote John 3:16? More importantly, are you living John 3:16? How can the world see the truth of John 3:16 in your life and in your actions?

5. What areas of your life need to be brought from darkness to light?

6. How are you treating the needy?

_____

_____

_____

_____

_____

JUDGES 19:1-20:48 JOHN 3:22-4:3 PSALM 104:24-35 PROVERBS 14:22-24	MAY **4**

Application:

1. For the second time in Judges we are told that Israel had no king. The Lord was supposed to be their king, but they refused to honor Him. How does your life reflect that God is your king?
2. The tribes of Israel react to the sin of Gibeah. How do you hold fellow believers accountable for their actions?
3. The armies of Israel continued the assault on Benjamin even after initial skirmishes were lost. Correcting sin and standing for righteousness is never easy! When are you tempted to allow sin when faced with resistance?
4. John humbly recognized that he must decrease that Jesus might increase. How are you decreasing in selfishness and ego that Jesus might increase?
5. Whoever believes in the Son has eternal life. Do you have eternal life based on your relationship with Christ? Take time today to make sure that you know the answer to this question.

JUDGES 21:1-RUTH 1:22 JOHN 4:4-42 PSALM 105:1-15 PROVERBS 14:25	MAY **5**

Application:

1. "...everyone did as he saw fit." (Judges 21:25) This line from Judges is descriptive of our culture. What must you do to break the mold and submit yourself and your family to God?

2. Naomi returns to Bethlehem bitter from the heartache in Moab. Are you harboring bitterness toward God or others? Ask God to root out the bitterness in your life because it will poison your spirit.

3. Despite fatigue and hunger, Jesus made a point to speak to the Samaritan woman at the well. Are you making efforts to engage those around you with the Gospel?

4. The woman at the well received grace from Jesus. Who do you know that is in need of God's grace today?

5. The people of the village discovered Jesus for themselves. Don't settle for the opinions of others, interact with Jesus personally! When are you tempted to accept the experience of someone else as your own encounter with Jesus?

RUTH 2:1-4:22 JOHN 4:43-54 PSALM 105:16-36 PROVERBS 14:26-27	MAY **6**

Application:

1. The story of Ruth and Naomi is a story of God's protection and provision. How has God protected you and your family?

2. Boaz showed great kindness to them and honored God's commands to care for the widows. How can you show kindness to the less fortunate?

3. Ruth, the Moabitess, was the great-grandmother of David. God allowed other ethnic groups to be involved in the lineage of the Messiah because the Messiah was for all people! How are you revealing the Good News to all people?

4. The man with the sick son "took Jesus at His word." (John 4:50) When do you have trouble taking Jesus at His Word? Ask God to help you trust Him.

5. How is your relationship with the Lord assembling a strong fortress for your children?

_____

_____

_____

_____

_____

1 SAMUEL 1:1-2:21 JOHN 5:1-23 PSALM 105:37-45 PROVERBS 14:28-29	MAY **7**

Application:

1. Hannah battled for her husband's affections with another woman. Men, does your wife battle for your affections with your hobby, career, or other "mistress"? Commit to give your affections fully to your spouse.

2. Hannah prayed honestly and earnestly to the Lord. Do you honestly place your interests before the Lord in prayer? What do you need to bring honestly to God today?

3. Hannah gave her son to the Lord's service. Parent, are you willing to submit your child to the Lord's service? What can you do to show your children that you want them to obey God above all else?

4. If Jesus could accomplish nothing apart from the Father, don't you think you need to remain connected to the Father? Take a look at your calendar. What changes do you need to make in order to remain connected to the Father?

5. Patience and understanding are linked. Do you see instances where your lack of patience hinders your ability to discern God's will in the world?

1 SAMUEL 2:22-4:22 JOHN 5:24-47 PSALM 106:1-12 PROVERBS 14:30-31	MAY **8**

Application:

1. Eli is rebuked for his failure to rebuke and discipline his sons. Parents, how do you discipline your children and show them right from wrong?

2. Pray the prayer of Samuel today, "Speak, for your servant is listening." (1 Samuel 3:10)

3. If you have accepted Christ, the promise of eternity given by Jesus is worth celebrating. Celebrate by telling someone about the promise of Jesus.

4. "Give thanks to the LORD, for he is good; his love endures forever." (Psalm 106:1) Thank God for His enduring love!

5. Are your bones rotting with envy? Confess the sin and receive the restoration of God.

1 SAMUEL 5:1-7:17 JOHN 6:1-21 PSALM 106:13-31 PROVERBS 14:32-33	MAY 9

Application:

1. No idols stand in the presence of God! What idols dominate your worship?
2. The story of the ark reveals that we cannot take the holiness of God for granted. When are you tempted to take God's holiness for granted?
3. Ebenezer means stone of help. Think back to the instances in your life where God has helped you. Thank Him for His activity in the past and the promised activity in the future.
4. Jesus displayed his power over nature when he walked on water to the disciples. How does that encourage you? How does it frighten you?
5. The Psalmist confesses that Israel forgot the activity of God. Let your Ebenezer's remind you of God's continued presence. Share your Ebenezer with a friend or co-worker today.

1 SAMUEL 8:1-9:27 JOHN 6:22-42 PSALM 106:32-48 PROVERBS 14:34-35	MAY **10**

Application:

1. Samuel led Israel, but it appears he forgot to lead his family. Fathers, how are you doing at leading your family? Mothers, are you investing enough energy in the spiritual growth of your family?

2. Peer pressure led the nation of Israel to beg for a king. If we are not careful, God will fulfill our requests. Are you asking God for something that contradicts His plan?

3. Do you seek miraculous signs as evidence of God's presence? While God works miracles, His activity in the simple things of life is more frequent. Thank God for working in the mundane aspects of your life.

4. Jesus, the Bread of Life, satisfies us. What do you need from God today to be satisfied?

5. At your job, how do you model righteousness?

_____

_____

_____

_____

_____

_____

1 SAMUEL 10:1-11:15 JOHN 6:43-71 PSALM 107:1-43 PROVERBS 15:1-3	MAY **11**

Application:

1. Saul hid behind the baggage at his own coronation. What responsibility are you shrinking from today?

2. God selected Saul to lead Israel. As we will see in the days to come, Saul is a flawed leader. Yet, God made him king over Israel. We must remember the instructions of the New Testament that we should pray for our political leaders, whether we agree with them politically or not.

3. The Bread of Life offers eternal life. If you have received this gift, take a moment today and thank God. If not, please take a moment and invite Jesus to come into your life, ask Him to forgive your sins, and give Him control of your life.

4. Following Jesus is never easy. Don't lose heart today when the trail steepens. Ask God for the strength and courage to persevere.

5. Offer gentle answers to everyone you meet today.

1 SAMUEL 12:1-13:23 JOHN 7:1-30 PSALM 108:1-13 PROVERBS 15:4	MAY **12**

Application:

1. Samuel was able to stand before the people with integrity at the end of his prophetic ministry. What habits must you cultivate so that you can stand with integrity at the end of your life?

2. Samuel says that he would not commit the sin of failing to pray for the nation of Israel. (1 Samuel 12:23) How can you pray for your country?

3. Saul's impatience proved to be his downfall. How is your impatience hindering your spiritual growth?

4. Initially Jesus' own family did not support His ministry. Don't give up if you are not receiving spiritual support at home. Cry out to Jesus for support, He knows how you feel.

5. Find ways to praise God "among the nations" today. (Psalm 108:3) You don't have to carry a guitar to the office, but you can tell others about the Mighty God you serve!

_____

_____

_____

_____

| 1 SAMUEL 14:1-52
JOHN 7:31-53
PSALM 109:1-31
PROVERBS 15:5-7 | MAY
13 |

Application:

1. Jonathan shows great courage and confidence in God when he attacks the Philistines. How is God calling you to show courage today?

2. While Jonathan courageously trusts God and wins the victory, Saul makes a superstitious vow that nearly costs Jonathan his life. How does your faith and prayer life resemble Saul? How does your faith and prayer life resemble Jonathan?

3. Are you sharing the Living Water of Christ with the world around you?

4. I would have loved to witness the two scenes described in John where they attempted to apprehend Jesus "but no one laid a hand on him." (John 7:44)

5. Meditate on the power of Christ contained in the human form of Jesus.

6. How do you accept the discipline/rebuke of others?

_____

_____

_____

_____

_____

1 SAMUEL 15:1-16:23 JOHN 8:1-20 PSALM 110:1-7 PROVERBS 15:8-10	MAY **14**

Application:

1. Partial obedience is disobedience! God desires obedience over sacrifice and ritual. In what areas of your life are you accepting partial obedience?

2. Samuel tried to select a king for Israel based on external indicators. How often we make the same mistake when we interact with others. Ask God to help you see others with His eyes.

3. Do you need to drop the stones of judgment that you are tossing at others?

4. How is the "light of the world" (John 8:12) shining through you?

5. How can you pursue righteousness? (Proverbs 15:9)

1 SAMUEL 17:1-18:4 JOHN 8:21-30 PSALM 111:1-10 PROVERBS 15:11	MAY **15**

Application:

1. David wasn't motivated by rewards or prestige, he wanted to honor God and defend God's glory. How can you defend God's glory today?
2. What giants taunt you today? God still empowers slingshots!
3. Jesus always relied on His Father. (John 8:28) What would you need to change in order to lead a Father-focused life?
4. Make a list of five things you can praise God for today.

_____

_____

_____

_____

_____

_____

_____

_____

_____

1 SAMUEL 18:5-19:24 **JOHN 8:31-59** **PSALM 112:1-10** **PROVERBS 15:12-14**	**MAY** **16**

Application:

1. The story of Saul is a tragedy. Saul allowed jealous anger to dominate his life. Who makes you jealous? Why?
2. Jonathan played the difficult role of mediator. At times we must work to bring about resolution in the hearts of the people around us. How can you serve as a mediator today?
3. What sins hold you in slavery? Confess and receive the freedom offered in Christ!
4. The Jews claimed they were righteous because of their ancestors. Jesus revealed that our spiritual inheritance is proven by our actions. What fruit in your life reveals the presence of God?
5. Have you informed your face of the joy that you have in Jesus? Let people see Jesus in your smile.

1 SAMUEL 20:1-21:15 JOHN 9:1-41 PSALM 113:1-114:8 PROVERBS 15:15-17	MAY **17**

Application:

1. Jonathan risked serious repercussions and displayed great integrity by supporting David. How can you show that same courage and integrity in supporting your friends?
2. Saul was driven by jealousy and anger. How do these emotions direct your life?
3. Do you assume that illness and difficulties are always a direct punishment for sin? Does this cause you to look down on others? Ask God to help you see people as He sees them.
4. The parents of the man Jesus healed were afraid of the religious leaders. How is the practice of your faith based on the fear of man? How is the practice of your faith based on the fear of God?
5. Do you praise God from the rising of the sun until it sets? Make a point to pause in the midst of your day today to praise God for His abundant blessings. Every hour spend at least one minute praising God

_____

_____

_____

_____

1 SAMUEL 22:1-23:29 JOHN 10:1-21 PSALM 115:1-18 PROVERBS 15:18-19	MAY **18**

Application:

1. David inquired of the Lord and sought the Lord's wisdom. How are you seeking God's wisdom today? How have you ventured out on your own wisdom?

2. While David fled the wrath of Saul, individuals displayed kindness and concern for David's cause. Who has come to your assistance in recent weeks? Thank God for them and then let them know that their actions are appreciated.

3. Do you recognize the voice of the Good Shepherd in your life? How can you better obey that voice?

4. Are you enjoying the full, abundant life that Jesus promised? How can you live the abundant life?

5. Do your actions typically glorify God or do they more frequently glorify you? What is your primary motivation?

| 1 SAMUEL 24:1-25:44 JOHN 10:22-42 PSALM 116:1-19 PROVERBS 15:20-21 | MAY 19 |

Application:

1. In the gospels, Jesus commanded his followers to love their enemies. David embodies that command in his treatment of Saul. How can you show respect to those who threaten you?

2. Abigail brokered peace between David and Nabal. She prohibited the otherwise inevitable conflict. How is God calling you to be a peacemaker today?

3. While the Bible does not directly confront David's polygamy, future stories certainly reveal the ill-effect of the King's practice. In the days to come note the repercussions in David's family.

4. "...no one can snatch them out of my hand." (John 10:28) This statement by Jesus is one of the clearest revelations of the eternal security of those who believe in Christ. Praise God that your salvation is centered on Christ's strength and not your own!

5. Which word provides the most appropriate description of your decision making: folly or understanding? Ask God for understanding!

1 SAMUEL 26:1-28:25 JOHN 11:1-54 PSALM 117:1-2 PROVERBS 15:22-23	MAY **20**

Application:

1. It is easy to miss the elapsed time of David's wilderness wandering. We read that David was in Ziklag for over a year which doesn't even take into account the previous wanderings. (1 Samuel 27:7) When have you become impatient with God's timetable? How did those situations turn out in the long run?

2. When the Lord did not answer Saul he turned to witchcraft. Lack of patience will lead us to listen to voices other than God's. When are you tempted to listen to a voice that isn't God's?

3. Jesus lingers before going to visit His friend Lazarus. While the delay might be considered indifference, it provides a forum for Jesus to work an incredible miracle. When have apparent delays and detours resulted in God's miraculous activity in your life?

4. Jesus spoke and Lazarus walked from the tomb. We serve The Resurrection and the Life! How does that reality impact your life today?

5. When seeking advice, do you try to find only those who will agree with you or do you try to discover a diversity of opinions?

| 1 SAMUEL 29:1-31:13
JOHN 11:55-12:19
PSALM 118:1-18
PROVERBS 15:24-26 | MAY
21 |

Application:

1. David was in a desperate situation. He was living with his enemies (the Philistines) when a raiding party captured his family and the families of his men. In the midst of potential mutiny, David found the strength of God and recovered the captured family members. David's situation provides us an example in difficult times. How do you turn to God on dark days?

2. Mary anointed the feet of Jesus. While Judas questioned this misuse of funds, Jesus explained that the gesture was appropriate. How can you give extravagantly to Jesus?

3. The people who placed branches on the road eagerly expected a Savior. They expected a military conqueror, Jesus proved to be so much more. How can you show similar enthusiasm for Jesus?

4. Do you take refuge in God or do you take refuge in the people around you? (Psalm 118:8) How have you been disappointed in man and encouraged by God?

5. What do your thoughts reveal about the sin in your heart?

2 SAMUEL 1:1-2:11 JOHN 12:20-50 PSALM 118:19-29 PROVERBS 15:27-28	MAY **22**

Application:

1. Even after Saul's death, David continues to seek the Lord's direction. In what areas are you tempted to be overconfident? Continue to seek God's face!

2. Where are you tempted to invest your resources in enhancing your earthly life? How can you better invest in eternity?

3. Religion seeks the approval of man; faith seeks the approval of God. When do you seek the approval of man?

4. Make a thanksgiving list, include specific blessings from God that you appreciate.

5. The mouth reveals the content of the heart. Does your mouth ever spew evil? What can you do to change that pattern?.

2 SAMUEL 2:12-3:39 JOHN 13:1-30 PSALM 119:1-16 PROVERBS 15:29-30	MAY **23**

Application:

1. Joab did not display honor or obedience in his murder of Abner. How do you allow bitterness to hinder your ability to honor God's commands?

2. Jesus took the role of the lowliest servant. The disciples had refused to stoop to that position. What tasks in the church or in the community are you unwilling to perform? Is God calling you to serve in those areas?

3. While the betrayal of Judas is an affront to our sensibilities, we often betray Jesus with our words and deeds. What do you need to remove from your life in order to stop betraying Jesus?

4. Do you hide God's word in your heart? Begin today by memorizing Psalm 119:11.

5. Would people describe you as cheerful? How can you display cheerfulness to strangers today?

| 2 SAMUEL 4:1-6:23
JOHN 13:31-14:14
PSALM 119:17-32
PROVERBS 15:31-32 | MAY
24 |

Application:

1. Even after David became king and experienced success, he continued to inquire of the Lord. (2 Samuel 5:23) In what area do you need to seek God's input today?

2. Uzzah's death reinforces God's holiness. How have you taken God's holiness for granted in worship? In life?

3. David danced before the Lord. While this ran contrary to the expectations of Michal, it reveals that "proper worship" can take many forms. How do you discern whether or not worship is pure?

4. How do others see Jesus in the way that you love your church family?

5. When the journey of life grows wearisome, remember that God is preparing an eternal abode that will eclipse anything on this earth! How does that news impact your attitude today?

6. Who gives you quality, constructive criticism? Who tends to tell you what you want to hear?

_____

_____

_____

_____

2 SAMUEL 7:1-8:18 **JOHN 14:15-31** **PSALM 119:33-48** **PROVERBS 15:33**	**MAY** **25**

Application:

1. Sometimes a no from God reveals a hidden yes! David would not build God's Temple, but one of his descendants would. God reveals that David would always have a son on the throne of Israel. Is God providing a hidden yes in an apparent no in your life?

2. David praises God in light of the blessings he has received and will receive. Take inventory of your blessings for few moments today. Thank God for each of them. Particularly consider the ways that He worked behind the scenes to guide you.

3. Our love for God is revealed (not earned!) through our obedience. What does your obedience reveal about your love for God?

4. God has provided the Holy Spirit to guide us in our journey of faith. How can you better yield to the Holy Spirit's guidance?

5. What "worthless things" (Psalm 119:37) compete for the attention of your eyes?

_____

_____

_____

_____

2 SAMUEL 9:1-11:27 JOHN 15:1-27 PSALM 119:49-64 PROVERBS 16:1-3	MAY **26**

Application:

1. The story of Mephibosheth reveals God's grace and mercy. David had every right to take Mephibosheth's life as a child of the former king. Instead, David gives Jonathan's son a place at the king's table. Take a few moments to praise God for giving you a place at His table!

2. David wasn't in the right place (at war) when he succumbed to temptation with Bathsheba. How are you placing yourself in the "wrong place" and thus opening the door to sin?

3. David compounds his sin by attempting to cover up the affair. Are you lying to cover up your sin? Come clean today and receive the cleansing available in confession.

4. How have your efforts to conceal sin injured others?

5. How is your connection to Christ? Apart from Jesus you can do nothing! Cultivate your connection.

6. One way to test your connection is to analyze your fruit production. What fruit are you producing for Christ?

7. God weighs your motives. (Proverbs 16:2) What motivates your actions?

_____

_____

_____

| 2 SAMUEL 12:1-31
JOHN 16:1-33
PSALM 119:65-80
PROVERBS 16:4-5 | MAY
27 |

Application:

1. Nathan had the courage and the God-given call to confront David with his sin. Is God calling you to confront other believers with their sin? Be courageous and follow the example of Nathan.

2. Confronted with his sin; David confessed and sought God's forgiveness. Do you need to seek God's grace today? Take time to repent.

3. While God forgave David's sin, David still suffered consequences. When have you experienced negative consequences for sinful acts?

4. God used Nathan to reveal David's sin to the king. God has given us the Holy Spirit. Don't overlook the inner voice of conviction that draws you back to God. What is the Holy Spirit speaking to you about?

5. If you are experiencing troubles in the world, take comfort because Jesus has overcome the world! How does this give you peace?

2 SAMUEL 13:1-39 JOHN 17:1-26 PSALM 119:81-96 PROVERBS 16:6-7	MAY **28**

Application:

1. As a consequence of his polygamy and other sins, David endures horrific situations with his children. Make no mistake, sin will have consequences. How are your current struggles the direct result of your sin?

2. David handles the rape of Tamar poorly. Though he is angry, he never punishes his son, Amnon. This leads to the rage and eventual rebellion of Absalom. In parenting and in life, we cannot ignore sin and conflict. Ignored sin and conflict will fester and infect. What conflict are you hoping will go away?

3. How does it encourage you to know that Jesus prayed for your protection in the world? (John 17:11)

4. Jesus prayed that his disciples and others who would follow them would be united in Him. Are you helping or hindering the unity of the body with your actions and attitudes? What can you do to foster unity in the body of Christ?

5. Pray the Psalm 119:81-96 today as a prayer of commitment to God's word and His ways!

_____

_____

_____

2 SAMUEL 14:1-15:22 JOHN 18:1-24 PSALM 119:97-112 PROVERBS 16:8-9	MAY **29**

Application:

1. Joab intervened between David and Absalom. Although this intervention did not ultimately end in restoration, Joab modeled peacemaking. How can you be a peacemaker in your home, on your job, or in the church?
2. As David flees Jerusalem, he finds some who are loyal and some who turn on him. Are you a loyal person? How do your friends know that they can count on you in times of desperate need?
3. Peter displayed courage when he struck the ear of the high priest's servant. However, he also displayed arrogance. This was not a part of Jesus' plan. Where are you displaying arrogance masked with courage? Remember, God's plans are not our plans and we have no right to step beyond God's plans.
4. Peter's arrogance quickly shifts to cowardice. When are you tempted to cowardice?
5. How do you allow the Word of God to direct your path?

2 SAMUEL 15:23-16:23 JOHN 18:25-19:22 PSALM 119:113-128 PROVERBS 16:10-11	MAY **30**

Application:

1. David displays great faith and restraint as he departs the city. He entrusts his fate to God. What circumstances in your life currently demand that type of trust on your part?

2. As the story of Absalom's rebellion unfolds, we are reminded that the advice we adhere to will ultimately shape our identity. Who is advising you? How would you evaluate that advice?

3. While trumping up charges to execute a sinless man, the Jewish authorities avoided ceremonial uncleanness by refusing to enter Pilate's palace. How do your religious practices focus on external appearances more than internal actualities?

4. As Jesus revealed, Pilate is ultimately an instrument of God's grand design. We must remember this as we consider our contemporary political climate. Rulers are ordained by God. Many times we cannot understand why certain rulers achieve power, but we submit ourselves to God's authority as we submit ourselves to their authority! Pray for your earthly leaders today.

2 SAMUEL 17:1-29 JOHN 19:23-42 PSALM 119:129-152 PROVERBS 16:12-13	MAY **31**

Application:

1. Absalom listened to advice that was intended to frustrate his efforts. Who, among your friends, consistently offers advice that goes against the Word of God?

2. Many people supported David during Absalom's revolt. In desperate times, it is important to realize that we are not alone. God has provided a church family to walk with us! Make a list of the people that you know will support you on the darkest days. Thank those people for their friendship.

3. The crucifixion accounts reveal numerous fulfilled prophecies. Every fulfilled Bible promise reminds us that God keeps His promises. What promises are you counting on most today?

4. What irony that Jesus, the Living Water, would cry out, "I am thirsty." (John 19:28) There are people around you every day who are thirsting for Living Water. How can you make a delivery?

5. What do you do to display zeal for the Word of God? (Psalm 119:139)

JUNE

2 SAMUEL 18:1-19:10 JOHN 20:1-31 PSALM 119:153-176 PROVERBS 16:14-15	JUN **1**

Application:

1. Absalom erected a monument to himself before his death. (2 Samuel 18:18) What type of legacy are you seeking to leave for yourself?

2. David doesn't handle Absalom's death well. It is likely that David's grief centered on his failure as a father. Parents, do you have regrets? Can any of those regrets be made right?

3. The miraculous is always hard to believe, that's the nature of miracles! The resurrection is no different. In spite of Jesus' predictions, the empty tomb baffles the disciples. Do you expect God to work miracles in your life? Expect the unexpected in your walk with Christ!

4. Jesus confronts the doubts of Thomas. What doubts does Jesus need to confront in your life?

5. The book of John was recorded to convince people that Jesus is the Christ. How can your life serve the same purpose?

2 SAMUEL 19:11-20:13 JOHN 21:1-25 PSALM 120:1-7 PROVERBS 16:16-17	JUN 2

Application:

1. Shimei deserved to die. He had disrespected the king and now the king was returning victorious. Yet David will not allow his warrior to end Shimei's life. Extending grace requires much more strength that exacting revenge. How can you imitate David's grace?

2. Joab jealously eliminates a potential rival in Amasa. Are there individuals that arouse jealousy within you? If so, ask God to help you overcome this jealousy.

3. Jesus restored Peter when he asked him three times to shepherd the flock. Are you in need of restoration today? Seek God's forgiveness and reconcile with your Creator!

4. Jesus did even more than we find recorded in the Gospel accounts. Take a few moments to praise God for those unknown miracles.

5. How can you avoid evil in every area of your life?

_____

_____

_____

_____

_____

2 SAMUEL 20:14-21:22 ACTS 1:1-26 PSALM 121:1-8 PROVERBS 16:18	JUN **3**

Application:

1. Sin always has consequences. The sin of Saul caused Israel to suffer through a famine. Where do you see consequences from sin in your life, in the life of your church, and in the life of your country?

2. It is unclear whether Mephibosheth sided with Absalom or not, but David again spares his life. How does David's treatment of Mephibosheth remind you of God's grace?

3. Notice the descriptive names that David attributes to God in the song recorded in 2 Samuel 22. How do you describe God? Make a list of five names of God.

4. What sort of witness are you providing for Christ in your community? How can you improve that witness?

5. When electing a successor to Judas, the early church cast lots. While this means of decision making might seem primitive (it was similar to rolling dice), it reveals that the church trusted God's sovereignty, (His ability to control all things for His purpose). What does your decision making reveal about your trust in God?

---

2 SAMUEL 22:1-23:23 ACTS 2:1-47 PSALM 122:1-9 PROVERBS 16:19-20	JUN **4**

Application:

1. David proclaimed that God had made his feet secure, like those of a deer. How do you find stability in God?

2. David's mighty men were renewed in their strength and valor. God needs mighty men (and women) to carry out His mission today. How can you stand courageously for God?

3. Peter proclaimed the first truly Christian sermon at Pentecost. Read Peter's words carefully and attempt to boil down the essentials of the Gospel. In three or four sentences write out the basic message of the gospel.

4. The conclusion of Acts 2 provides a snapshot of the early church. What can you do to make your church resemble the snapshot provided in Acts?

5. In Psalm 122, David rejoices at the opportunity to experience the presence of God at the Temple. Do you have the same type of joy at entering God's presence in worship or prayer? If not, what can you do to cultivate that type of enthusiasm?

_____

_____

_____

_____

2 SAMUEL 23:24-24:25 ACTS 3:1-26 PSALM 123:1-4 PROVERBS 16:21-23	JUN **5**

Application:

1. The sin of the census involved David's pride. Where does pride tend to creep into your life?

2. Sacrifice always costs us something; that is the nature of sacrifice. Our walk with God will always require sacrifice on our part. What have you sacrificed for Christ? What is God calling you to sacrifice?

3. The name of Jesus is the source of the disciple's healing power. How have you witnessed the power of Christ's name?

4. Who do you know that is longing for times of refreshment? (Acts 3:19) Ask God to give you a heart for those who are suffering from spiritual thirst.

5. Today concentrate on making your words pleasant so that you might encourage and instruct those around you.

1 KINGS 1:1-53 ACTS 4:1-37 PSALM 124:1-8 PROVERBS 16:24	JUN **6**

Application:

1. David apparently forgot to mold his sons into men after God's own heart. How can you encourage your children to seek God?

2. David didn't interfere with Adonijah and correct his misbehavior. Parents, how can you correct your children today? Do not assume that misbehaving children will correct themselves. That is your job!

3. Joab turned on David in his later days. Have you ever experienced this type of betrayal? Have you ever betrayed a friend? Where possible, seek to restore broken relationships.

4. Salvation is found in Christ alone. (Acts 4:12) This message runs contrary to the cultural agenda, but it is the foundational truth of God's Word. Redemption comes through Christ! In what other person or practice do you seek salvation?

5. Do people recognize that you have been with Jesus? How is that characteristic evident in the way you interact with others?

6. When are you tempted to obey man rather than God?

_____

_____

_____

1 KINGS 2:1-3:2	JUN
ACTS 5:1-42	
PSALM 125:1-5	**7**
PROVERBS 16:25	

Application:

1. As David prepares for death he gives Solomon a blessing and a challenge. Dads how are you blessing and challenging your sons to walk in the Lord's ways?

2. The frightful story of Ananias and Sapphira warns against false pretenses in worship. When are you tempted to put on a "Christian happy mask" in worship and prayer?

3. The disciples show great boldness. After they are arrested they obey God and return to the city to proclaim the Good News. Ask God to give you courage to share the gospel.

4. We will experience persecution as Christians. The disciples rejoiced when beaten for the cause of Christ. Ask God to help you find joy in times of persecution.

5. Don't expect God to adjust His plans to meet your expectations. Where do you need to yield your plans to God's?

_____

_____

_____

_____

_____

1 KINGS 3:3-4:34 ACTS 6:1-15 PSALM 126:1-6 PROVERBS 16:26-27	JUN **8**

Application:

1. You might not be a king, but you can ask God for wisdom. We all need God's wisdom, spend a few moments asking God to grant you wisdom.

2. Solomon was given great wealth, wisdom and honor. What would you do with those gifts? What are you doing with the talents, treasures and abilities that God has entrusted to you?

3. "The people of Judah and Israel were as numerous as the sand on the seashore." (1 Kings 4:20) This fulfills the promise given to Abraham a thousand years earlier. Praise God because He keeps His promises!

4. Even the early church faced conflict. What is your role in church conflicts? How can you strive to resolve conflict?

5. Psalm 126 describes the joy of Israel as they returned to the land of promise. Take a few moments today to rejoice in the eternal home that God has promised to you.

1 KINGS 5:1-6:38 ACTS 7:1-29 PSALM 127:1-5 PROVERBS 16:28-30	JUN 9

Application:

1. What Temple-sized task has God commissioned you to complete? What Temple-sized tasks can you help others complete?

2. Stephen reminds his accusers of God's faithfulness over the years. What is your "salvation history"? We must remember God's work in the past as we trust God for His work in the future.

3. What are you trying to accomplish on your own strength? (Psalm 127:1)

4. How can you protect your lips from gossip?

1 KINGS 7:1-51 ACTS 7:30-50 PSALM 128:1-6 PROVERBS 16:31-33	JUN **10**

Application:

1. We are given a hint that something is amiss in Solomon's life. He invested more time on his palace (13 years) than he did on the Temple (11 years). Where are you investing more time and energy in your personal interests over God's Kingdom plans?

2. Solomon utilized individuals skilled in craftsmanship to construct the Temple (and his palace). If you are able to build or create, find ways to utilize that talent for the glory of God!

3. In his defense, Stephen tells the "whole story" of God's activity. Sometimes it is necessary and appropriate to provide people with more than a three minute gospel presentation. It is important that we be familiar enough with God's Word that we can tell His story.

4. Thank God for the blessings and provisions you have received when you obeyed Him.

5. Ask God to help you cultivate patience and control your temper

1 KINGS 8:1-66 ACTS 7:51-8:13 PSALM 129:1-8 PROVERBS 17:1	JUN 11

Application:

1. Pray that God's glory will fill you and your church family.
2. God keeps His promises. Make a list of God's promises that you have seen fulfilled.
3. Stephen calls his accusers "stiff-necked." It took incredible boldness on the part of Stephen to call out his accusers. How can you display that type of boldness in your conversations?
4. Could you accurately be described as stiff-necked? What could you change in your life in order to change that description?
5. Are you spending so much time earning money that you neglect to enjoy life? Write down three things you can do today to enjoy life. Then, do them!

| 1 KINGS 9:1-10:29
ACTS 8:14-40
PSALM 130:1-8
PROVERBS 17:2-3 | JUN
12 |

Application:

1. Solomon is reminded that the blessings of God are contingent on obedience. When things go awry in our lives, we should first consider our obedience to God. How are you walking in His ways?
2. Have you ever tried to purchase God's favor through actions or finances? Meditate on the results of those attempts.
3. The Ethiopian could not understand the gospel without Philip's help. What can you do to make the Good News clear to those who don't understand it?
4. Meditate on the reality that God has forgiven your filthy transgressions!
5. What does God discover when he tests your heart?

_____

_____

_____

_____

_____

_____

1 KINGS 11:1-12:19 ACTS 9:1-25 PSALM 131:1-3 PROVERBS 17:4-5	JUN **13**

Application:

1. While polygamy is practiced in the Bible, it is certainly not prescribed. The families of David and Solomon reveal the potential pitfalls of polygamy. Make a list of the consequences that David's family experienced as a result of this sin.

2. When we intermingle unwittingly with the things of the world, we will often be corrupted. How is the world corrupting you?

3. Solomon's intermarriage led him to worship despicable gods. (Molech and Chemosh required child sacrifice!) A small crack in the believer's life can quickly become a giant chasm! Where are you allowing cracks in your spiritual life?

4. Ananias boldly accepted the Lord's call to befriend Saul, who had persecuted and killed believers. What dangerous tasks are you being called to undertake?

5. "Saul spent several days with the disciples in Damascus." (Acts 9:19) While we often think of Paul's conversion as a brief event, we discover that He was discipled over time by other followers of Christ. Who is discipling you and who are you discipling?

6. The psalmist speaks of being still and quiet before God. Practice stillness and quiet before God today.

1 KINGS 12:20-13:34 ACTS 9:26-43 PSALM 132:1-18 PROVERBS 17:6	JUN **14**

Application:

1. Jeroboam tempted his people with convenient worship. How are you tempted to make worship convenient and comfortable when it is intended to be challenging?

2. The man of God spoke boldly against the idolatry of Jeroboam. How is God calling you to speak boldly about idolatry in the lives of those around you?

3. Barnabas reached out to Saul even though the other disciples feared the convert. Are there people around you who are struggling to make radical life change based on the call of Christ? How can you help them?

4. What does Acts convey when you read that the church was "living in the fear of the Lord." (Acts 9:31). What implications does that have for your church?

5. Has God blessed you with grandchildren? Thank Him for bestowing this honor on you.

_____

_____

_____

_____

_____

1 KINGS 14:1-15:24 ACTS 10:1-23 PSALM 133:1-3 PROVERBS 17:7-8	JUN **15**

Application:

1. Nothing is hidden from the sight of God. Perhaps you should spend some time today dealing with the things you have pretended He could not see

2. While Jeroboam offered false idols, Rehoboam offered God and idols. This tactic is still practiced by many today. They claim faith in Christ, but they tack on additional gods to their floundering faith. What god have you added to your faith?

3. Asa risked strained family relationships to stand up for righteousness. How willing are you to take risks for your faith?

4. God revealed to Peter that all food was permissible. This declaration drew fire from legalists in the fledgling Christian community. Where do you see legalism in your church and your life?

5. When have you experienced the joy of unity described in Psalm 133?

1 KINGS 15:25-17:24 ACTS 10:24-48 PSALM 134:1-3 PROVERBS 17:9-11	JUN **16**

Application:

1. Although delayed, Jeroboam received punishment for his sin. Have you been frustrated that some seem to get away with sin? Remember, sin always carries consequences.

2. The widow at Zarephath showed faith and kindness. How can you display these same traits?

3. Peter would not allow Cornelius to worship him. Is there anyone that you admire so deeply that it borders on worship? Do you subconsciously seek the worship of others?

4. The message God revealed to Peter through Cornelius reminds us that the whole world needs the gospel. What are doing personally to reach that goal?

5. When offended, do you overlook the offense or do you scurry to your friends and spark the gossip cycle? If you gravitate toward gossip, ask God to protect you from this temptation.

_____

_____

_____

_____

_____

1 KINGS 18:1-46 ACTS 11:1-30 PSALM 135:1-21 PROVERBS 17:12-13	JUN **17**

Application:

1. Obadiah faced a crisis of belief. He had already risked his life and now Elijah asked him to take another step of faith. How is God challenging you to continue the journey of faith?

2. How are you wavering between the opinion of God and the opinion of the world? What can you do to get off the fence?

3. Pray that God will send the fire of revival that will ignite a flame even greater than Elijah's altar.

4. It is easy to criticize another's ministry when looking from the outside. Be certain that you know the truth before you criticize the laborer. Also, critique privately, not publicly.

5. Think of five praiseworthy things that God has done this week. Now, Praise the Lord!

1 KINGS 19:1-21 ACTS 12:1-23 PSALM 136:1-26 PROVERBS 17:14-15	JUN **18**

Application:

1. The greatest attacks often come on the heels of our greatest victories. If you have experienced recent successes, ask God to protect you!

2. Satan perpetuates the myth that the people of God never get depressed. Rather than believing this lie, we should recognize depression and seek God's help. Sometimes this help takes the form of Christian friends or counselors. Don't suffer in silence!

3. Elisha's sacrifice of the oxen marked a decided turning point in his walk with God. Have you reached that point? When was it? If you have not, make it today?

4. The church was praying for Peter's release, yet they were shocked by Peter's presence. When has God surprised you with answered prayers?

5. God's love endures forever. Thank God by telling someone how you have experienced His enduring love.

1 KINGS 20:1-21:29 ACTS 12:24-13:15 PSALM 137:1-9 PROVERBS 17:16	JUN **19**

Application:

1. Ahab attempted to give in to the demands of the bully, Ben-Hadad. Bullies are never satisfied. When are you tempted to succumb to the demands of bullies?

2. In spite of his wealth, Ahab wanted what was not his. This desire led to murder. What are you coveting?

3. God called the church at Antioch to send out Barnabas and Saul. Churches must be sending agents not sitting places. How is God using your church to advance the Kingdom? Who is God sending? Is it you?

4. The Holy Spirit is the guide for the church and the missionaries. Does the Holy Spirit have that sort of influence on your life? What can you do to yield to the Holy Spirit's influence?

5. How can you seek wisdom over wealth?

1 KINGS 22:1-53	JUN
ACTS 13:16-41	**20**
PSALM 138:1-8	
PROVERBS 17:17-18	

Application:

1. Ahab refused to listen to the prophets that spoke against him. Are you willing to listen to those who tell you things that you are not excited to hear? What prophetic voice do you need to heed today?

2. While Jehoshaphat typically followed God, he made an unwise allegiance with the wicked Ahab. Are you partnering with anyone who is obviously ungodly? Seek to sever this relationship as it will lead to ruin.

3. Through Christ we are justified of our sins. Spend time thanking God for this unmerited gift of grace.

4. Paul traces the redemption of God, revealed fully in Christ, through the history of Israel. As you read the Old Testament, remember that all of the events lead to the cross.

5. How can you stand with your friends in times of adversity?

6. Thank God that He provided a brother in Christ to rescue you from adversity.

2 KINGS 1:1-2:25 ACTS 13:42-14:7 PSALM 139:1-24 PROVERBS 17:19-21	JUN **21**

Application:

1. Ahaziah sought the advice of the god of Ekron. Where do you seek advice?

2. People talk of going out in a "blaze of glory." Elijah's exceptional exit certainly fits that description. While your exit might not be as dramatic, your arrival will be just as spectacular. Meditate for a few moments on what it will be like to arrive in the presence of God.

3. Paul and Barnabas offered Truth to the people of Pisidian Antioch. Unfortunately, some of the religious leaders were jealous and they defended the status quo by stirring up dissent. When are you tempted to reject Truth in order to defend the status quo?

4. While some reject the disciples and some accept them, it seems that the vast majority lie somewhere in the middle, uncertain and confused. The religious leaders targeted the undecided and sought to turn them against the cause of Christ. The same occurs today. How can you help provide clarity to the undecided that are facing spiritual attack today?

5. Meditate on Psalm 139:13. What emotions do you experience when you are reminded that God created you?

2 KINGS 3:1-4:17 ACTS 14:8-28 PSALM 140:1-13 PROVERBS 17:22	JUN **22**

Application:

1. God provided oil for the woman facing desperate poverty. The only limit to God's gift was the amount of jars the woman collected. How are you limiting God's ability to work through you by your lack of faith?

2. The Shunammite woman displayed hospitality to Elisha. Who needs a touch of hospitality from you?

3. Paul and Barnabas bypassed the praises of the people, who assumed they were gods, and reflected the glory to God. When you serve God, are you seeking the praise of man or do you serve for His Glory? Confess to God the places where you serve for personal gain.

4. Paul picked himself up after having stones pummel his body and returned to proclaim the gospel to the very people who had hurled the rocks. What does this teach you about holding a grudge?

5. How do the people around you benefit from your cheerful heart?

_____

_____

_____

_____

2 KINGS 4:18-5:27 ACTS 15:1-35 PSALM 141:1-10 PROVERBS 17:23	JUN **23**

Application:

1. God challenges us to believe that the dead will rise again. Do you trust God's power over death? How does that belief impact your life?
2. Naaman almost missed the Lord's healing because the "solution" was too simple. When have you been guilty of overcomplicating God's commands?
3. Gehazi's greed resulted in leprous skin. How is your greed impacting your life?
4. The early church rejected the temptation to place stumbling blocks in the path of new converts. Rather than requiring new Christians to first become Jews, they wisely recognized that faith in Christ superseded circumcision. How does you church place cultural stumbling blocks in the path of those coming to Christ?
5. Make Psalm 141:3-4 your prayer today.

_____

_____

_____

_____

_____

2 KINGS 6:1-7:20	JUN
ACTS 15:36-16:15	
PSALM 142:1-7	**24**
PROVERBS 17:24-25	

Application:

1. Elisha's servant could not see the heavenly protection that surrounded Elisha. Ask God to help you "see" the spiritual protection that He has given you.

2. The lepers who discovered that the army of Aram had fled determined that they should share the good news of God's deliverance. How can you share the Good News of God's deliverance with others?

3. If you doubt the Lord's ability, you will rarely witness the Lord's power. Ask God to help you expect amazing things from Him.

4. Barnabas took John Mark's side against Paul. Barnabas was an encourager who was willing to give the young man a second chance. Who can you give a second chance today?

5. Paul followed the Lord's direction and headed for Macedonia. Where is God directing you today?

_____

_____

_____

_____

_____

2 KINGS 8:1-9:13	JUN
ACTS 16:16-40	
PSALM 143:1-12	**25**
PROVERBS 17:26	

Application:

1. The kings of Israel and Judah refuse to obey and honor God. Time and again they choose the path of least resistance rather than following God. As you look at your life, do you typically obey or do you, like the leaders of Israel and Judah, follow your own path? Ask God to strengthen you, that you might follow His path!

2. Beaten and bloodied, chained to each other in the bellows of a Roman prison, Paul and Silas praised God. What an unlikely location for worship. When have you praised God in the trials?

3. Over and over again, the disciples repeat the refrain, "Believe in the Lord Jesus, and you will be saved" (Acts 16:31). Have you placed your faith in Jesus? How are you sharing your faith in Jesus?

4. Make this your prayer today, "Teach me to do your will."

2 KINGS 9:14-10:31	JUN
ACTS 17:1-34	
PSALM 144:1-15	**26**
PROVERBS 17:27-28	

Application:

1. You reap what you sow! In this gruesome section from 2 Kings many evil leaders, like Jezebel, receive their punishment. Don't pretend that your sin will not find you.

2. The Bereans received the message of Paul with great eagerness and tested it against Scripture. Not everyone who writes a book or preaches a sermon has a true word from the Lord! How do you examine the messages you hear or read?

3. Examine Paul's message at Areopagus notice how the disciple preaches the same message of Christ crucified in a unique manner in order to engage the Athenians. Ask God to give you wisdom in ways that you can share your faith.

4. Sometimes silence increases your intelligence exponentially! Ask God to help you hold your tongue today.

2 KINGS 10:32-12:21 ACTS 18:1-22 PSALM 145:1-21 PROVERBS 18:1	JUN **27**

Application:

1. Jehoiada courageously preserved the proper king (Joash) and destroyed the wicked queen. Where is God calling you to stand up for what is right, even when the situation is dangerous?

2. Joash broke with the tradition of his family, and sought to honor God. If you are attempting to make a break from a heritage of unrighteousness, take comfort in the example of Joash. Ask God to give you the strength and courage of Joash.

3. Paul seems to rise above potential rivalries and establish strong teams. He partnered with Priscilla and Aquila to further the kingdom. Don't look for rivals in the kingdom of God. Instead seek teammates! Who has God provided for you as ministry partners?

4. Praise God today for his grace and compassion. (Psalm 145:8)

5. Do most of your passions and desires involve selfish ends? One of the greatest stumbling blocks in our faith is destroying the selfish nature that rises up within us. Ask God to help you in your ongoing battle with self.

_____

_____

_____

2 KINGS 13:1-14:29	JUN
ACTS 18:23-19:12	
PSALM 146:1-10	**28**
PROVERBS 18:2-3	

Application:

1. Due to the wickedness of Israel's kings, God allowed the nation to experience oppression. If you find yourself living under the yoke of oppression, ask God if you are living in sin. (It is not a guarantee that your struggles are a result of your sin, but if they are, wouldn't you like to know!)

2. We often ask why God punishes the innocent. Wouldn't a better question be, why doesn't God punish the guilty? That would be all of us! Thank God for His grace.

3. Priscilla and Aquila model discipleship with Apollos. Rather than viewing Apollos as a threat or rebuking him publicly, they quietly took him aside and "explained to him the way of God more adequately." (Acts 18:26) Who needs this type of gentle steerage in your life? If you need it, who might be willing to provide it?

4. Paul wasn't afraid or ashamed to dialogue with scoffers. How can you engage others for the cause of Christ? We should not be in attack mode, but we must be watchful and ready!

5. Do you enjoy hearing yourself talk? Ask God to help you spend more time listening and less time talking.

2 KINGS 15:1-16:20	JUN
ACTS 19:13-41	**29**
PSALM 147:1-20	
PROVERBS 18:4-5	

Application:

1. Even the descriptions of the kings who honor God often include a notation that the high places were not removed. These reforming kings stopped short in their revival efforts and retarded the spiritual growth of Israel. What are you holding onto that is holding you back?

2. Ahaz offered his son as a sacrifice to the false gods of the land. What are you sacrificing? Your time? Your family? Your money? To which god is your sacrifice directed? Remember, the wrong god always demands the wrong sacrifice!

3. The sons of Sceva attempted to do the things of God without the power of God and they received a beating for it. What are you trying to do on your own strength?

4. How can you hold the name of Jesus in high honor in your speech, in your worship, in your prayer?

5. Revealing idolatry will always cause conflict. Where do you need to reveal idols in the lives of others?

| 2 KINGS 17:1-18:12
ACTS 20:1-38
PSALM 148:1-14
PROVERBS 18:6-7 | JUN
30 |

Application:

1. The sins committed in secret never escape the All-Seeing eyes of God. What sins do you think you are concealing?
2. The label stiff-necked seems so descriptive and appropriate. How does it fit you?
3. Hezekiah destroyed the bronze snake that ended the plague in the desert because the people were worshiping this figure instead of the Lord who sent healing. How are you worshiping past markers of God instead of God?
4. Paul balanced rebuke with encouragement. How are you at striking that balance?
5. Paul reminds the Ephesians to help the weak. In your life, who could use a helping hand today?

JULY

2 KINGS 18:13-19:37 ACTS 21:1-17 PSALM 149:1-9 PROVERBS 18:8	JUL **1**

Application:

1. Like Goliath, Sennacherib taunted Israel and Israel's God. Who or what taunts you and your God today? Remember that God is greater than any obstacle that you face.
2. In utter desperation Hezekiah cried out to God. Don't wait until the situation is dire to involve Almighty God! Cry out to God with your struggles today.
3. Paul's farewell tour reveals the fellowship and love of the early church. What can you do to facilitate this kind of community in your church family?
4. Are you prepared to give your life for the cause of Christ? Are you prepared to live your life for the cause of Christ?
5. The best way to silence a gossip is to remove their audience. Ask God to tune your ears to recognize gossip so that you can steer clear of it.

| 2 KINGS 20:1-22:2
ACTS 21:18-36
PSALM 150:1-6
PROVERBS 18:9-10 | JUL
2 |

Application:

1. While we do not have sufficient time or space to fully address the issue, this passage indicates that Hezekiah's prayer altered the Lord's original plan. Don't give up! Keep praying!

2. Arrogance always catches up with us. Hezekiah showed off his possessions because he forgot that they belonged to the Lord. Which possessions threaten to possess you?

3. "He forsook the LORD... and did not walk in the way of the LORD." (2 Kings 21:22) Could that sad epitaph be written of you? What can you change to make that less descriptive of you?

4. Obey the command of the Psalm, praise the Lord!

_____

_____

_____

_____

_____

_____

| 2 KINGS 22:3-23:30
ACTS 21:37-22:16
PSALM 1:1-6
PROVERBS 18:11-12 | JUL
3 |

Application:

1. The people of Israel had literally lost the commands of God. Josiah drew the attention of the people to God's written Word. As you are reading the Word of God this year, draw the attention of others to this life-giving word!
2. The Word of God brings revival to the people of God. Allow the Word to bring revival to your heart, that you might infect others with the power of God!
3. Paul utilizes his testimony to proclaim the Good News of Christ. Who needs to hear your story of the Savior?
4. Do you place more faith in your bank account than you place in God? Ask God to adjust your attitude toward money.

2 KINGS 23:31-25:30 ACTS 22:17-23:10 PSALM 2:1-12 PROVERBS 18:13	JUL **4**

Application:

1. The evil of Manasseh cannot be fully undone by the righteousness of Josiah. Evil has far-reaching effects. What type of legacy are you leaving your family?

2. The kingdom of Israel was short-lived. It started with such potential and promise when Joshua led the nation into Canaan. Even the greatest beginnings can be spoiled by rebellious disobedience! Where does sin thwart God's design for you and your church family?

3. Paul reveals the hypocrisy of the religious leaders. Legalists tend to emphasize the laws that they keep best or the ones that best suit their interests. Ask God to help you avoid the trap of legalism.

4. Ironically, the Roman officials protect Paul from the Jewish mob. Sometimes help comes from unexpected sources. Who might God use to help you?

5. Make a concerted effort to listen before you speak today.

_____

_____

_____

_____

_____

1 CHRONICLES 1:1-2:17 ACTS 23:11-35 PSALM 3:1-8 PROVERBS 18:14-15	JUL 5

Application:

1. The genealogies record the history of the nation and provide a framework for the kingship that follows. As you read, note that each individual played a part, either positive or negative in the history of Israel and in God's plan for the redemption of man. What part are you playing?

2. God's message to Paul is simple, "Take courage!" (Acts 23:11) Perhaps you need to heed this admonishment today as well. Take courage in God's strength.

3. The Roman officials work to keep Paul safe from the Jews. God utilizes those in authority even when we might not admire or appreciate them. How can you show respect to the authorities in your life?

4. Thank God for the moments in your life when He has been your shield. (Psalm 3:3)

5. How do you seek knowledge?

1 CHRONICLES 2:18-4:4	JUL
ACTS 24:1-27	
PSALM 4:1-8	6
PROVERBS 18:16-18	

Application:

1. Paul is on trial for His faith. If placed on trial for your faith, what evidence would be utilized to prove that you believe in Christ?

2. Paul spoke of righteousness and self-control before a leader who had stolen the wife of his brother. How can you stand up for righteousness?

3. Anger can lead us to sin if not handled appropriately. Do you control your anger or does your anger control you? Ask God to help you with your anger.

4. Are you a giving person? Look for opportunities to bless others by giving to them.

_____

_____

_____

_____

_____

_____

| 1 CHRONICLES 4:5-5:17 ACTS 25:1-27 PSALM 5:1-12 PROVERBS 18:19 | JUL 7 |

Application:

1. Like Jabez, pray for God's blessings.
2. Paul's determined defense attracted King Agrippa. How are people drawn to you by your thoughtful description of your faith?
3. Lay your requests before God today expecting a response from Him.
4. Are you nursing grudges? Ask God's forgiveness and then seek reconciliation.

1 CHRONICLES 5:18-6:81 ACTS 26:1-32 PSALM 6:1-10 PROVERBS 18:20-21	JUL **8**

Application:

1. The Reubenites, Gadites, and half tribe of Manasseh experienced victory because they trusted God. Do you believe that God is able to overcome the obstacles in your life? List those obstacles and ask God to overcome them.

2. Paul repeated the story of his conversion to any who would listen. How often do you recount the events of your salvation? Ask God to provide opportunities to share your faith story.

3. Paul sought to persuade Agrippa and the entire court. Paul is persuasive but not pushy. How can you present the gospel in persuasive ways?

4. How do your words give life or death?

1 CHRONICLES 7:1-8:40	JUL
ACTS 27:1-20	
PSALM 7:1-17	9
PROVERBS 18:22	

Application:

1. The genealogical record reminds us that the people of God are not immune to adversity. The presence of difficulty is not always a sign of God's absence. How might the difficulties in your life be evidence of God's presence?

2. Paul's experience at sea reinforces the sentiment of the Old Testament reading. Paul courageously obeyed God's instructions only to find himself as a prisoner in a storm at sea.

3. Thank God for the instances when He has been a refuge in your life.

4. Join the psalmist in praying for an end to violence.

5. If you have been blessed with a Godly spouse, thank God for them.

1 CHRONICLES 9:1-10:14 ACTS 27:21-44 PSALM 8:1-9 PROVERBS 18:23-24	JUL **10**

Application:

1. The men of Jabesh Gilead courageously rescued the bodies of Saul's family. Often honorable actions require sacrifice and danger. How can you show honor?

2. Saul's sad epitaph points out his failure to inquire of the Lord. While David constantly sought God's direction, Saul refused to seek God's wisdom. Don't make Saul's mistake! How can you seek God's wisdom today?

3. Paul shows concern for his captors in the shipwreck. How can you show kindness to your enemies?

4. Take a moment today to observe the skies: watch the sunset, gaze at the stars, or consider the power of the sun. Praise the Creator for His handiwork.

5. Do you have true friends or mere acquaintances? Thank your friends for being true friends.

1 CHRONICLES 11:1-12:18 ACTS 28:1-31 PSALM 9:1-12 PROVERBS 19:1-3	JUL **11**

Application:

1. While it is easy to attribute David's rise to power to his sharp leadership, his military power or his shrewd political maneuvers, the Bible is clear that David prospered because the Lord was with him. What evidence in your life reveals that the Lord is with you?

2. The mighty men and others came to David as he fled from Saul. They sensed that David was God's anointed and placed their allegiance with the future king. Who are you following? Are they worthy of your trust?

3. Paul's imprisonment enabled him to share the gospel unhindered in Rome. From this political and cultural center, God used Paul to advance the Kingdom. Remember that the adversity in your life might be a part of God's plan to fulfill His purpose!

4. Zeal and enthusiasm do not prove that your cause is just. Intensity does not necessarily indicate wisdom. Where are you attempting to conceal a lack of wisdom with enthusiasm?

5. When have you blamed God for your own folly?

_____

_____

_____

1 CHRONICLES 12:19-14:17 ROMANS 1:1-17 PSALM 9:13-20 PROVERBS 19:4-5	JUL 12

Application:

1. Those who joined David sided with a righteous cause. What righteous cause needs your support?
2. The anger of the Lord directed at Uzzah offers a fierce reminder of the Lord's holiness. Are there any areas in which you take the holiness of God for granted?
3. The book of Romans explains the gospel of Jesus. How would you describe the gospel (Good News) of Jesus?
4. Are you ashamed of the gospel of Christ? Think about your daily conversations and habits. What can you do to help people see the gospel in you or hear the gospel from you?
5. Are you overtly or covertly deceiving your family, friends or co-workers? Confess your deceit and ask for God's assistance in consistently speaking truth.

1 CHRONICLES 15:1-16:36 ROMANS 1:18-32 PSALM 10:1-15 PROVERBS 19:6-7	JUL **13**

Application:

1. Kenaniah led the musicians because he was skilled in singing. What skills do you need to employ for the Lord's service?

2. David led Israel to celebrate the placement of the ark in Jerusalem. Sometimes we are too busy to celebrate the victories that God provides. What blessings do you need to celebrate today?

3. Are there any objects, hobbies, or individuals that you idolize before God?

4. Check your life against the list of wickedness Paul provides. Note any similarities and ask God to remove the wickedness in your life.

5. Do you feel that God is distant? Cry out as the Psalmist does and discover that God's presence is never contingent on your circumstances.

1 CHRONICLES 16:37-18:17 ROMANS 2:1-24 PSALM 10:16-18 PROVERBS 19:8-9	JUL **14**

Application:

1. Priests, gatekeepers and musicians received assignments from David. What is your role in the community of faith? How are you sharing your gifts?

2. It is tempting to do something for God. David wanted to build a Temple, but God said no. Are you trying to "do something" that God has instructed you to leave alone? We can never honor God while disobeying his instructions.

3. Do you have a tendency to look down on those around you, casting judgment on their sins while ignoring your own? Ask God to replace your judgmental spirit with a merciful spirit.

4. God will judge your secrets. What are trying to hide from God?

5. How can you aid the fatherless and oppressed?

_____

_____

_____

_____

_____

1 CHRONICLES 19:1-21:30 ROMANS 2:25-3:8 PSALM 11:1-7 PROVERBS 19:10-12	JUL 15

Application:

1. David succumbed to the temptation of numbers. In a numbers-infatuated society we must remember that growth is not always measured numerically. Where do you tend to be too concerned about numbers? (church attendance, bank account, bottom line at work, etc.)

2. If you doubt your forgiveness based on earthly consequences, remember that sometimes even forgiven sin bears physical consequences. Thank God for forgiveness and ask for His strength to endure the consequences.

3. Paul warns the Romans against external displays of worship that overlook the internal transformation that God desires. When are you tempted to focus on the external displays of faith?

4. If we think grace gives us the freedom to sin, we have completely missed the purpose of grace and the cost of Christ's sacrifice. Meditate on Christ's sacrifice and how that impacts your view of sin.

5. When do you have trouble overlooking the offenses of others?

1 CHRONICLES 22:1-23:32 ROMANS 3:9-31 PSALM 12:1-8 PROVERBS 19:13-14	JUL **16**

Application:

1. David set aside all Solomon would need for the Temple. Parents, what are you setting aside for your children for the generations to come? We often think about the inheritance we will leave, but how can we leave our children the tools that they need to be obedient to God?

2. You are a sinner. The next time that you are repulsed by a public sin, remind yourself that your sins are just as grotesque in the eyes of God. Thank God that He saves all who will call on Him!

3. Do you ever play the gold-star game where you imagine that God gives gold stars based on all of your good works. The book of Romans destroys the premise of this game and reminds us that grace cannot be earned. Repent of trying to earn salvation and thank God for giving it to you!

4. Do you quarrel with your spouse or your co-workers? Would people describe you as a leaky faucet? (Proverbs 19:13)

_____

_____

_____

_____

1 CHRONICLES 24:1-26:11 ROMANS 4:1-12 PSALM 13:1-6 PROVERBS 19:15-16	JUL **17**

Application:

1. This passage sheds light on the value of family in Jewish culture. The musicians were supervised by their fathers. Parents, your family will naturally gravitate in different directions. What are you doing to draw your family together?

2. God credited Abraham with righteousness based on his faith. Abraham did not earn righteousness by obedience. The obedience sprang out of faith. Are you trying to manufacture obedience without faith? It will never work!

3. David's early desperation turns to faithful hope in this Psalm. If you understand David's desperate tone, then keep trusting, keep rejoicing, and keep singing!

4. Do you listen to the instructions of others? Too many times we barrel through life like a two-year old, unwilling to heed the warnings of those who have already experienced life. Seek out an elder who can speak wisdom into your life today.

1 CHRONICLES 26:12-27:34 ROMANS 4:13-5:5 PSALM 14:1-7 PROVERBS 19:17	JUL **18**

Application:

1. God promised Abraham that his descendants would be more numerous than the sand on the seashore. While Abraham didn't live to see the promise fulfilled, the record in Chronicles reveals the impressive development of the nation of Israel. God keeps His promises. What promises do you believe God might fulfill after your lifetime?

2. A ceasefire brings joy on both sides of the battle. Through Christ's actions we are no longer at war with God. Rejoice because you can lay down your sword and quit fighting the Lord.

3. In what areas has God called you to suffer for his cause?

4. Are you showing kindness to the poor in tangible ways? What are you willing to give up that others might have food and water?

1 CHRONICLES 28:1-29:30 ROMANS 5:6-21 PSALM 15:1-5 PROVERBS 19:18-19	JUL 19

Application:

1. David offers direct instructions to Solomon, complete with a warning against disobedience. Parents, how are you providing your children direct guidelines for Godly living?

2. David knew that the Temple would be an arduous task for Solomon. He warned against fear and discouragement. What task overwhelms you today? Ask God to give you courage to face the task.

3. Challenged by the king, the people gave generously to the work of the Temple. How are you giving generously of your resources? (Remember, your time and talents are a part of your resources also.)

4. Do you have someone who knows you well? Jesus knows you better than that person, in fact, He knows you better than you know yourself. Yet, in spite of all He knows, He was willing to die in your place. Take some time to praise Him for the sacrifice!

5. Where does sin still rule your life?

6. Parents do not abdicate your responsibility to correct and instruct your child. While they will have many friends, they will only have, at most, two parents.

2 CHRONICLES 1:1-3:17 ROMANS 6:1-23 PSALM 16:1-11 PROVERBS 19:20-21	JUL **20**

Application:

1. Solomon passed up earthly wealth to request earthly wisdom. Ask God to grant you the wisdom to accomplish His purpose in your life.
2. When are you tempted to take grace for granted?
3. Are any parts of your life still in rebellion against God? Submit to the authority of Christ in every area of your life.
4. Are you a slave of God? What evidence in your life supports this assertion?
5. The psalmist reminds that God will not leave us. (Psalm 16:10) As you go through your day, remember that God goes with you.

_____

_____

_____

_____

_____

_____

_____

| 2 CHRONICLES 4:1-6:11
ROMANS 7:1-13
PSALM 17:1-15
PROVERBS 19:22-23 | JUL
21 |

Application:

1. The Hebrew people knew how to celebrate God's victories. What should you celebrate today? Invite some friends over and celebrate God's blessings.

2. Reflect on the Ten Commandments (Exodus 20:1-17). How does God's law reveal your sinfulness? Take some time to dwell on your depravity. We cannot understand God's grace until we have recognized our sin.

3. Do you live by the Spirit or by the "letter of the law?" Take a few minutes to ponder this vital question.

4. Have you ever felt that everyone was against you? David obviously struggled with these issues, too. Follow the great king's lead and recognize that God will not forsake you.

_____

_____

_____

_____

_____

_____

_____

2 CHRONICLES 6:12-8:10 ROMANS 7:14-8:8 PSALM 18:1-15 PROVERBS 19:24-25	JUL **22**

Application:

1. Solomon prayed, "There is no God like you." (2 Chronicles 6:14) Pray that prayer to God today and meditate on His uniqueness.

2. God's presence interrupted Solomon's worship service. Pray that God will interrupt your worship with the power of His presence. Ask God to stir within His church and ignite a revival among His people.

3. Solomon did not complete the Temple overnight. God might be calling you to a God-sized task that can only be completed on a God-sized timetable. What long-term project is God calling you to complete?

4. Paul bemoans his constant failure to live in God's holiness. How do you battle the tension between your sinful nature and God's call to holiness?

5. Satan accuses the followers of God, attempting to berate them into guilt-laden lives. But Paul reminds us that there is no condemnation for those who belong to Christ Jesus. When the accuser attacks, remind him that you are free in Christ!

6. How are you feeding your sinful nature? How are you feeding your spiritual nature?

| 2 CHRONICLES 8:11-10:19
ROMANS 8:9-25
PSALM 18:16-36
PROVERBS 19:26 | JUL
23 |

Application:

1. The splendor of Solomon's reign should remind us of God's promises to Abraham. God promised that He would make Abraham into a great nation. God always fulfills His promises. Thank God for His faithfulness.

2. Rehoboam's failure reminds us of the value of wise counsel. Do you tend to surround yourself with people who tell you what you want to hear or do you seek the wisdom of those who disagree?

3. If you accept your sinfulness as human nature, you deny the activity of the Spirit in you. Remember, the power of the resurrection can transform your life and overcome your sinful nature. Ask God to empower you in your battle against sin.

4. As you pray today, thank your Father for adopting you into His family.

5. David praises God for rescuing Him. Are you in need of rescue today?

2 CHRONICLES 11:1-13:22 ROMANS 8:26-39 PSALM 18:37-50 PROVERBS 19:27-29	JUL **24**

Application:

1. The Levites left everything to remain on Rehoboam's side. What are you willing to sacrifice in your quest to stand up for what is right?

2. The Lord allowed his people to endure chastisement in order to draw them to Himself. God will do the same in your life. Is God trying to reveal something to you about your disobedience? Don't ignore his discipline!

3. Sometimes our most painful prayers are inaudible to human ears. At those times the Spirit intercedes and interprets for us. Don't be afraid to pray in groans and tears.

4. What do you fear? In Romans 8, Paul reminds us that nothing can separate us from God's love. Cast your fears into the depths of God's love.

2 CHRONICLES 14:1-16:14	JUL
ROMANS 9:1-24	
PSALM 19:1-14	**25**
PROVERBS 20:1	

Application:

1. Asa had the courage to stop the tide of spiritual rebellion in Judah. Are you willing to stand against that same tide today?

2. Many moved to Judah during the reign of Asa because they recognized that this ruler was seeking to honor God! Who do you know that is attempting to advance the kingdom? How can you partner with them in their efforts to advance the Kingdom?

3. The courage and commitment of Asa's younger years wanes as the king ages. He begins to trust in diplomacy over God's activity. How do you sense your fervor for God fading? Ask God to restore the passion in your life and avoid the arrogance of Asa.

4. Paul warns the Jewish people, his people, that they have missed God's Messiah. Like Israel, we cannot stake our spiritual inheritance on past-tense faith. When do you feel tempted to reside on your past?

_____

_____

_____

_____

2 CHRONICLES 17:1-18:34 ROMANS 9:25-10:13 PSALM 20:1-9 PROVERBS 20:2-3	JUL **26**

Application:

1. Jehoshaphat destroyed the high places, which were a stronghold of spiritual darkness. What strongholds linger in your life? What habits, attitudes, and actions divert you from God?

2. A catalyst for the revival under Jehoshaphat was the teaching of the Law. When people fail to consult the Word of God, they begin to conjure ill-conceived images of God. Do you base your understanding of God on His Word?

3. Why doesn't Jesus return? Paul suggests that Jesus patiently awaits the repentance of His people. What are you doing to accelerate the spread of the Gospel of repentance?

4. Have you ever called on the name of the Lord, in order that you might be saved? If so, spend some time thanking Him. If not, meditate on Romans 10:9-11.

5. David speaks of those who trusted in horses and chariots. (Psalm 20:7) While the temptation to trust in chariots has passed, the temptation to trust technological advancements still exists. When are you tempted to trust technology?

| 2 CHRONICLES 19:1-20:37
ROMANS 10:14-11:12
PSALM 21:1-13
PROVERBS 20:4-6 | JUL
27 |

Application:

1. Jehoshaphat made a poor choice in associating with Ahab and Ahaziah. In your life, who hinders your relationship with God?

2. Often the people of God experience victory in battle without lifting a weapon. Too often we attempt to win the victory in our strength rather than allow Almighty God to handle the situation. In what situation are you working on your own when you need to trust God?

3. "… how can they hear without someone preaching to them?" (Romans 10:14) Paul's question still reverberates today. Who needs to hear the Good News from you?

4. Are you willing to spend time in self-reflection? Plunge into the deep waters and allow God to give you the wisdom to draw out the purposes of your heart. (Proverbs 20:5)

2 CHRONICLES 21:1-23:21 ROMANS 11:13-36 PSALM 22:1-18 PROVERBS 20:7	JUL **28**

Application:

1. Jehoram veered from the righteous path his father, Jehoshaphat, had blazed. How are you honoring your family's legacy of faith? If your family's legacy of faith started with you, how can you leave a strong legacy for your children?

2. It would have been easy for Jehoiada to go along with the wicked reign of Athaliah. However, he courageously took a stand and led a revolt. Doing the right thing often requires courage and sacrifice. In what situation is God calling you to display courage and sacrifice by standing for Him?

3. We cannot comprehend or understand the riches of God's wisdom and knowledge. When we struggle to understand God's ways, we must remember that a god we could completely comprehend would not deserve our worship. Make a list of God's unfathomable qualities and spend time praising Him for the things you cannot comprehend.

4. In light of Christ's proclamation on the cross, "My God, my God, why have you forsaken me?" (Psalm 22:1) How does Christ's sacrifice provide clarity to this Psalm?

2 CHRONICLES 24:1-25:28 ROMANS 12:1-21 PSALM 22:19-31 PROVERBS 20:8-10	JUL 29

Application:

1. After Jehoaida's death, Joash turned from God. Is your faith contingent on outside influences (a spouse, a parent, etc.)? Faith cannot be absorbed by osmosis! You must cultivate your own faith.
2. Amaziah worshipped the impotent idols of the Edomites. Which idols receive your worship?
3. How would you rate yourself as a living sacrifice?
4. Do you, like most people, have an elevated view of self? Don't allow the disease of self to erode your soul and your church. Ask God to continue to transform you into His image by replacing your self-centered nature with the sacrificial nature of Christ.
5. Do you live in harmony with others? Think about your relational history. Do your relationships or acquaintances typically end in quarrels? Strive to live in peace.

2 CHRONICLES 26:1-28:27 ROMANS 13:1-14 PSALM 23:1-6 PROVERBS 20:11	JUL **30**

Application:

1. Uzziah received spiritual instruction from Zechariah. Who is instructing you? (This could be a friend, minister, or even a celebrity whose books you read.) If you can identify a spiritual instructor, then ask yourself if that individual is providing sound Biblical instruction. If not, try to find someone who can speak Truth into your life.

2. Pride always facilitates a fall. How is pride plotting to trip you up?

3. Adversity led Ahaz farther from God. How do you respond to adversity? Do you cling closely to God or do you flee from His presence?

4. Failure to submit to human authority reveals a failure to submit to divine authority. Do you live in submission to the authority figures in your life? Boss? Government officials? Pastor?

5. What are you doing about your continued debt to love others? (Romans 13:8)

6. The Shepherd Psalm conveys peace and stillness. Allow your Shepherd to remove you from the busyness of the day so that He can provide you with the nourishment you need.

_____

_____

_____

2 CHRONICLES 29:1-36 ROMANS 14:1-23 PSALM 24:1-10 PROVERBS 20:12	JUL **31**

Application:

1. Before Hezekiah's reign, the Temple had been abandoned. Pray that the people of God will not abandon the worship of God.
2. As Hezekiah reveals, God can resurrect His work. How does God want to use you to ignite His church?
3. Do you believe that all of your views on church and worship are sacred? While Truth must be maintained, we must be considerate of those whose interpretations vary.
4. Ask God to give you clean hands and a pure heart.
5. How is God at work in the world around you? Make a concerted effort to look for God's activity today.

AUGUST

2 CHRONICLES 30:1-31:21 ROMANS 15:1-22 PSALM 25:1-15 PROVERBS 20:13-15	AUG 1

Application:

1. Most ridiculed Hezekiah's invitation to return to God but "some men of Asher, Manasseh, and Zebulun humbled themselves and went to Jerusalem." (2 Chronicles 30:11) What choices to serve God will cause ridicule and rebuke in your life today?

2. Corporate worship gave the Israelites courage to smash the sacred stones and cut down the Asherah poles. Do not forsake corporate worship; you need the courage it provides! If you do not have a church family, ask God to direct you to a place where you can be a part of His community.

3. Pray that God will instill unity in your church.

4. Paul displays a clear sense of calling and purpose. What is your purpose? What has God called you to accomplish for His kingdom?

2 CHRONICLES 32:1-33:13 ROMANS 15:23-16:9 PSALM 25:16-22 PROVERBS 20:16-18	AUG 2

Application:

1. In spite of Hezekiah's faithfulness, Sennacherib invaded Judah. Faithful actions do not always guarantee peace and prosperity. If you are experiencing turmoil, continue to trust God.

2. Do you struggle with a proud heart, as Hezekiah did? Repent of your pride and humble yourself before God!

3. Manasseh ignored the pleas of the prophets. What warning or rebuke from God are you ignoring?

4. Paul asked the church in Rome to cover his missionary efforts in prayer. How can you pray for missionaries? Ministers?

5. Allow God to be your refuge today. Find the protection and provision that only God can offer.

2 CHRONICLES 33:14-34:33 ROMANS 16:10-27 PSALM 26:1-12 PROVERBS 20:19	AUG 3

Application:

1. The story of Manasseh's repentance reveals the depths of God's grace. Don't give up on your wayward family members; don't lose heart in your prayers. God can lead even the hardest heart to repentance!

2. The law led the king and the nation to revival and repentance. Pray that the contemporary church would experience a revival fueled by the Word of God.

3. Unlike most of the kings in Israel, Josiah was faithful from start to finish. Resolve to finish your faith with as much vigor as you started your faith. Ask God to empower you for this journey.

4. Paul's list at the end of Romans reminds us that each individual plays an important role in the work of the church. What is your role?

5. How have you accidently or intentionally caused division in the church of God?

2 CHRONICLES 35:1-36:23 1 CORINTHIANS 1:1-17 PSALM 27:1-6 PROVERBS 20:20-21	AUG **4**

Application:

1. Josiah reinstituted the Passover. Israel had forgotten this feast which reminded them of God's deliverance. Don't neglect the observance of the Lord's Supper, lest you forget the sacrifice that God provided in Christ.

2. The exile is a sad blot in the history of Israel. God had given His people so much, yet they turned from him, neglecting His gifts. When are you tempted to neglect or ignore God's gifts?

3. Those who attempt to divide the church commit treason against God. Pray that God will protect His church from divisiveness.

4. How do your actions, words and attitudes bring the people of God together?

5. The Corinthian church worshipped at the cult of personality; some preferred Paul, others Apollos, and others Peter. The church has only one Lord, His name is Jesus! Ask God to help you resist the temptation to worship at the cult of personality.

| EZRA 1:1-2:70
1 CORINTHIANS 1:18-2:5
PSALM 27:7-14
PROVERBS 20:22-23 | AUG
5 |

Application:

1. Cyrus allowed the exiled Jews to return to their homeland. God used the Persian king to set His people free. All kings and rulers are under the authority of God! Pray for your government leaders today.

2. God did not forget His children in exile. When have you feared that you were forgotten by God?

3. As was the case in Corinth, the Gospel of Jesus still provokes cynics. It seems too simple, too good to be true. Continue to pray that this simple story of Good News will continue to overwhelm the world!

4. Paul claims that the cross is the power of God. (1 Corinthians 1:18) How is the cross the power of God in your life?

5. The Corinthians liked oratory, flowery public speaking. Apparently Paul's speech wasn't polished by Corinthian standards. Paul encourages the Corinthians to consider the content and substance of his messages. How have you allowed the expectations of the world to influence your opinion of your pastor?

_____

_____

_____

EZRA 3:1-4:23	AUG
1 CORINTHIANS 2:6-3:4	
PSALM 28:1-9	6
PROVERBS 20:24-25	

Application:

1. Can you imagine the joy the Jewish people must have experienced when they were once again able to offer sacrifices in Jerusalem. Most probably presumed they would die before they returned to their homeland. Even when things are bleak, trust that God will keep His promises.

2. Whenever we seek to do God's work, there will always be opposition. Who is opposing you as you seek to do God's work? Don't mistake opposition for God's absence!

3. How does the Spirit of God impact your life?

4. Think back to the early stages of your walk of faith. How have you grown in Christ? Thank God for the changes that have been completed and those still in progress.

5. Notice the names that the Psalmist attributes to God. What names do you attribute to God?

_____

_____

_____

_____

_____

EZRA 4:24-6:22	AUG
1 CORINTHIANS 3:5-23	
PSALM 29:1-11	7
PROVERBS 20:26-27	

Application:

1. The leaders attempting to restore Israel faced opposition in obeying God's direction. What opposition do you face in obeying God's will? How can you persevere in that opposition?

2. It is dangerous when the people of God confuse the servant of God with God. If you have elevated an individual to an even playing field with God, ask God's forgiveness.

3. God will judge not only our actions but the attitudes that motivated the action. Take a few moments to consider, what motivates your service?

4. Think back to the reverence that the Jewish people displayed for the Temple. Paul says that you are the Temple of God. What does Paul mean by that statement? How does it impact your life?

EZRA 7:1-8:20	AUG
1 CORINTHIANS 4:1-21	
PSALM 30:1-12	**8**
PROVERBS 20:28-30	

Application:

1. While spiritual leaders should never be confused with God, they are important to the work of God as seen in the life of Ezra. How do you show respect for the servants of God?

2. Take a few moments to reflect on the gifts you have been given. How are you doing as a steward of those gifts?

3. Do you live such a life that you could, like Paul, encourage people to imitate you? Ask God to help you live in such a way that people will see Christ in you!

4. Notice the deliverance of God that is praised in Psalm 30. What type of deliverance do you need today?

5. Do you respect the opinions of the gray-headed among you? They have earned those gray hairs with experience; you should listen to their counsel. Schedule a time to sit down and learn from someone whose experience exceeds your own.

_____

_____

_____

_____

_____

EZRA 8:21-9:15 1 CORINTHIANS 5:1-13 PSALM 31:1-8 PROVERBS 21:1-2	AUG 9

Application:

1. Ezra was ashamed to ask the king for further assistance because he had told the king that God would provide. How can you display dependence on God, so that others can see your trust in Him?

2. Ezra was appalled at the sin of Israel. Are you appalled by the sins of Christians in your country? Pray a prayer of confession as Ezra did. Assume a posture of repentance and ask for God's mercy on your nation.

3. Where does sexual immorality threaten to invade your life?

4. Paul indicates that Christians should be more concerned with sin inside the church than sin outside the church. (1 Corinthians 5:12) What sins need to be addressed within your community of faith?

5. God controls the hearts of kings and rulers. Pray for your leaders.

_____

_____

_____

_____

_____

EZRA 10:1-44 1 CORINTHIANS 6:1-20 PSALM 31:9-18 PROVERBS 21:3	AUG **10**

Application:

1. It is not enough to simply confess sin. We must also repent and turn from our sinful actions. Develop action steps for turning away from your sin.

2. Church people have a bad reputation for taking their conflicts outside the church. This destroys the witness of the church in the community. Are there any festering conflicts between you and another church member or Christian that need to be addressed? Set up a time to meet with those individuals and seek reconciliation.

3. Grace enables us to live in freedom, but freedom should never abuse grace. How are you abusing God's grace?

4. How does your body convey the holiness of God?

5. God prefers action over ritual. How are you acting out your faith?

| NEHEMIAH 1:1-3:14
1 CORINTHIANS 7:1-24
PSALM 31:19-24
PROVERBS 21:4 | AUG
11 |

Application:

1. Like Ezra, Nehemiah is shaken to his core by the failures of Israel. Ask God to increase your sensitivity to sin.

2. Nehemiah made a bold request of the king in obedience to God. What is God calling you to do that will require boldness?

3. Nehemiah was a charismatic leader who rallied the nation of Israel to a cause. However, Nehemiah constantly points out that God is directing the rebuilding efforts. Ask God to help you distinguish between charismatic leadership and Godly leadership.

4. Day-to-day living wears on your marriages like dirt on an engine. Do an engine clean-out and renew your commitment to your spouse! Compile a list of things you can do to strengthen your connection to your mate.

5. Read Psalm 31 and spend a few moments meditating on the greatness of God's love.

_____

_____

_____

_____

_____

NEHEMIAH 3:15-5:13	AUG
1 CORINTHIANS 7:25-40	
PSALM 32:1-11	**12**
PROVERBS 21:5-7	

Application:

1. The dream of rebuilding the wall required work and action. Are you willing to work to build up your church or are you waiting for others to carry the load? Find ways to get involved with your church family.

2. Following God's leadership often invokes opposition. Who is opposing your obedience to God? Don't cower to the taunts of men when God has called you to a task!

3. Nehemiah led the people to pray and work. The two must remain balanced. How do you maintain the balance between prayer and action?

4. Singleness is sometimes viewed as a secondary option in our culture. Paul applauds those who are able to live single lives because they are less encumbered in their service to God. What is your attitude toward singleness?

5. This Psalm is a call to repentance. What are you keeping from God? What sin needs to be confessed?

| NEHEMIAH 5:14-7:73
1 CORINTHIANS 8:1-13
PSALM 33:1-11
PROVERBS 21:8-10 | AUG
13 |

Application:

1. Nehemiah made personal sacrifices to see the work on the wall completed. What is God calling you to sacrifice in order to advance the kingdom?

2. Nehemiah refused to meet with detractors because he was focused on the wall. Don't get caught up in the clouds of dissension, instead focus on your ministry!

3. The people who left Babylon to rebuild Jerusalem were pioneers. They courageously left the familiar to repopulate the home land. Is God calling you to a courageous adventure?

4. God is not the answer to a trivia question; He is a living entity that desires an ongoing relationship with you. How are you tempted to value knowledge about God over knowing God? What can you do to insure that you pursue God more than knowledge about Him.

5. How do your actions cause others to stumble?

NEHEMIAH 7:73-9:21 1 CORINTHIANS 9:1-18 PSALM 33:12-22 PROVERBS 21:11-12	AUG **14**

Application:

1. The Word of God is always a prominent part of any revival of God. How are you allowing the Word to impact your life and actions?

2. At times we should mourn, as Ezra and Nehemiah did when confronted with sin, and at times we should celebrate, as the people did when confronted with God's Word. What circumstance in your life calls for mourning? What circumstances call for celebration?

3. If you are feeling distant from God, list the ways that God has worked in your life. This will remind you of God's grace and draw you back into his presence.

4. Paul exemplifies one who ignored his own rights in order to serve others. In what instances are you so consumed with getting what you deserve that you miss the opportunity to minister to others?

5. We are tempted to place our hope in jobs, money, education, and the government. God is the only one worthy of your hope! Spend a few minutes thanking God that your hope is secure in Him.

_____

_____

_____

NEHEMIAH 9:22-10:39	AUG
1 CORINTHIANS 9:19-10:13	
PSALM 34:1-10	**15**
PROVERBS 21:13	

Application:

1. The people of Israel continued to commit themselves to God in covenants. Do you need to make a fresh commitment to God today? Take a moment and write out your commitment to God.

2. We must be willing to step outside our comfort zone in order to reach those who are not like us. Who is God calling you to reach? What step of discomfort will that require?

3. What prize are you pursuing? Are you focused on worldly prizes or are you focused on eternal rewards?

4. Do some self-analysis. If Satan were to attack you, where would the devil strike? Where are the chinks in your armor?

5. Do you hear the cries of the hurting? If you can't hear them, ask God to tune your ears. If you can hear them, ask God to give you the strength to serve.

_____

_____

_____

_____

_____

NEHEMIAH 11:1-12:26	AUG
1 CORINTHIANS 10:14-33	
PSALM 34:11-22	**16**
PROVERBS 21:14-16	

Application:

1. The Israelites honored those who were willing to enter the city. Sometimes the faith community needs individuals to make sacrifices. What sacrifices can you make for your faith family? Also, how can you honor and affirm the sacrifices of others?

2. It is easy to get lost in genealogical records, but this account tells the story of Israel's return from exile and the fulfillment of God's promise to His people. How does fulfillment in the past impact your faith today?

3. Paul forfeited his own rights in order to reach others. What rights do you need to forfeit?

4. "Follow my example, as I follow the example of Christ." (1 Corinthians 11:1) What needs to change in your life before you can say that with confidence to others?

_____

_____

_____

_____

_____

_____

NEHEMIAH 12:27-13:31 1 CORINTHIANS 11:1-16 PSALM 35:1-16 PROVERBS 21:17-18	AUG **17**

Application:

1. Worship expresses and increases the joy of the faith community. How do you find joy in worship?
2. Nehemiah actively opposed sin. He drove people away and threatened to lay hands on them (and not in the prayerful way!) How can you take a stand against sin today?
3. What would you need to do to make Christ the head of your life? Your marriage? Your family? Your church?
4. What worldly pleasures hamper your heavenly pursuits? What pleasures, habits and addictions should you surrender to God?

ESTHER 1:1-3:15 1 CORINTHIANS 11:17-34 PSALM 35:17-28 PROVERBS 21:19-20	AUG **18**

Application:

1. God's name is not mentioned in the book of Esther but his fingerprints are revealed throughout the book. How is God working in the background of your life?

2. Mordecai drew the ire of Haman because he refused to worship another man. When are you tempted to worship someone rather than the God of the universe?

3. Paul admonished the church at Corinth for fostering division. How can you encourage your fellow believers rather than picking sides against them?

4. The Lord's Supper is an exercise in fellowship and community. It reminds us that we are all in need of Christ's sacrifice. Whenever you begin to harbor a grudge with another believer, remember that Christ died for them just as he died for you. Don't wait for the next Lord's Supper observance to make things right with others, take time today to restore and renew any relationships that need healing.

5. Wives, are you quarrelsome and ill-tempered? What can you do to lay aside your quarrelsome spirit and foster harmony with your spouse?

ESTHER 4:1-7:10 1 CORINTHIANS 12:1-26 PSALM 36:1-12 PROVERBS 21:21-22	AUG **19**

Application:

1. Esther was providentially placed in the king's palace to preserve the nation of Israel. What has God strategically positioned you to do that no one else can accomplish?

2. Esther's actions required boldness and faith. How can you encourage others who are exercising boldness and faith?

3. What are your spiritual gifts? How are you employing those gifts?

4. How can you encourage someone in your faith family today who utilizes their spiritual gifts to build up the body? Try to think of the individuals who don't typically receive recognition.

| ESTHER 8:1-10:3
1 CORINTHIANS 12:27-13:13
PSALM 37:1-11
PROVERBS 21:23-24 | AUG
20 |

Application:

1. Think back to moments when God providentially protected you as He did the Jewish people. Spend some time thanking God for His sovereign protection.

2. Mordecai was esteemed because he spoke up for the good of his people. How can you speak up for the good of others?

3. Are you jealous of the gifts that others possess? Confess your jealousy to God and thank Him for giving you the gifts you have been given.

4. God is concerned with our ministry and our motive. Allow the Holy Spirit permission to reveal your motivations in ministry.

5. Could the description of love in 1 Corinthians 13 be applied to your life? If not, what needs to change?

_____

_____

_____

_____

_____

_____

JOB 1:1-3:26 1 CORINTHIANS 14:1-17 PSALM 37:12-29 PROVERBS 21:25-26	AUG **21**

Application:

1. Does it make you uncomfortable that God suggests Job to Satan? Would God suggest you as a faithful servant?
2. Do you worship God for the things that God has given you or do you worship God because He is God?
3. How do you encourage those who are facing trials? Job's wife offers a poor example while Job's friends displayed wisdom in their silence.
4. How are you using your gifts to build up and encourage other believers?
5. What cravings threaten to destroy you?

_____

_____

_____

_____

_____

_____

_____

| JOB 4:1-7:21
1 CORINTHIANS 14:18-40
PSALM 37:30-40
PROVERBS 21:27 | AUG
22 |

Application:

1. Job's friends follow their silence with sermons. They failed when they opened their mouths because they started putting words in the mouth of God! When do you find yourself putting words in God's mouth?

2. When have you experienced the despair of Job? Take comfort in the fact that God does not hide from the hurt of humanity.

3. Paul's description of the church seems different than our contemporary expressions of church. In Paul's description, the believers brought something to worship, rather than expecting something from worship. How does this truth adjust your current approach to worship?

4. Is God's law in your heart? More practically, how is God's law in your actions and attitudes?

JOB 8:1-11:20
1 CORINTHIANS 15:1-28
PSALM 38:1-22
PROVERBS 21:28-29

AUG

23

Application:

1. The book of Job is interesting in that the "speeches" by Job's friends are later rebuked by God. As you read these speeches, consider how they misrepresent God.

2. Job's words are laced with faith-filled questioning. He doesn't doubt God; He is trying to understand God. Be sensitive in your conversations with individuals who are hurting. Sometimes the venom of bitterness masks the foundation of faith. Help them find their foundation.

3. What aspects of the gospel are the most important according to Paul?

4. How does the resurrection affect your daily life? How should the resurrection impact your daily life?

JOB 12:1-15:35 1 CORINTHIANS 15:29-58 PSALM 39:1-13 PROVERBS 21:30-31	AUG **24**

Application:

1. Job's statement drips with sarcasm, "Doubtless you are the people, and wisdom will die with you!" (Job 12:2) Although Job's friends meant well, they actually made the situation worse. When do the words you use for the purpose of encouragement actually make things worse? Why does this happen?

2. How does the company you keep influence your character?

3. If you are growing tired of your finite mortal body, praise God for the imperishable body that is to come!

4. Spend some time praising God for the victory over death available through Christ.

5. What steps can you take to make God a critical advisor in your decision making process.

_____

_____

_____

_____

_____

_____

| JOB 16:1-19:29
1 CORINTHIANS 16:1-24
PSALM 40:1-10
PROVERBS 22:1 | AUG
25 |

Application:

1. Job say, "My days have passed, my plans are shattered, and so are the desires of my heart." (Job 17:11) Sometimes God allows us to experience the depths of despair so that we can find His strength. Can you relate to the despair of Job? Have you ever discovered God's strength in the midst of despair?

2. Paul advises the Corinthians to take up a collection for the church in Jerusalem. Why would Paul advise them to give to others? How can giving benefit the giver?

3. What steps do you need to take so that you can stand firm in the faith?

4. Make a list of God's wonders. Then, work to bring up God's wonders in your conversations.

5. Do you have a good name in the community? At your workplace? Why? Or Why not?

JOB 20:1-22:30 2 CORINTHIANS 1:1-11 PSALM 40:11-17 PROVERBS 22:2-4	AUG **26**

Application:

1. The dialogue between Job and his friends continues to escalate. At some point it seems that both sides begin to focus on "proving their side." When do you allow conversations to escalate due to personal pride? Ask God to keep your pride in check.

2. How can you use the comfort God has offered you to provide comfort for others?

3. Paul viewed hardship as God's reminder for complete dependence. How is God reminding you that His grace is sufficient?

4. How can you show respect to others as God's creation?

_____

_____

_____

_____

_____

_____

_____

JOB 23:1-27:23 2 CORINTHIANS 1:12-2:11 PSALM 41:1-13 PROVERBS 22:5-6	AUG **27**

Application:

1. Job seeks God through his pain, he doesn't relent. If you are experiencing pain, don't give up on God. Keep seeking His strength!

2. What would the people you see on a daily basis say about your holiness and sincerity?

3. The Corinthians started doubting the Gospel because Paul was forced to change his travel plans. When do you allow your convictions in the gospel to be impacted by the actions of man?

4. Parents, how are you teaching your children to follow Jesus?

_____

_____

_____

_____

_____

_____

JOB 28:1-30:31	AUG
2 CORINTHIANS 2:12-17	
PSALM 42:1-11	**28**
PROVERBS 22:7	

Application:

1. How are you growing in your search for wisdom?

2. Paul refers to an "open door" in 2 Corinthians 2:12. While at times we must await an open door for God's specific instructions, we must not wait on general obedience. For example, all Christians are called to live holy lives, share their faith, be a part of a community of believers, etc. It would be silly and disobedient to wait for an "open door" to obey God's general instructions. Is there anything you are waiting to do that God has already provided you approval for in His Word?

3. How is the aroma of Christ projected by your presence?

4. Are you bound by the shackles of debt? Covenant with God and ask for his guidance in escaping the stronghold of indebtedness.

_____

_____

_____

_____

_____

_____

JOB 31:1-33:33 2 CORINTHIANS 3:1-18 PSALM 43:1-5 PROVERBS 22:8-9	AUG 29

Application:

1. Job took a proactive stance against lust. (Job 31:1) Make a similar commitment and seek God's strength to fulfill it.

2. Elihu offers advice to Job and his three friends. Elihu is not rebuked by God for his comments so they seem to offer a better model for helping the hurting. How does Elihu differ from the others?

3. Who are you discipling?

4. Just as we are to carry the aroma of Christ, we are also to display the glory of Christ. How do you display a God-glow to those you meet? How do they see Christ reflected in your words and deeds?

5. Are you sowing wickedness? Repent and ask God to help you sow seeds of righteousness.

JOB 34:1-36:33 2 CORINTHIANS 4:1-12 PSALM 44:1-8 PROVERBS 22:10-12	AUG **30**

Application:

1. We often believe, like Job, that God has treated us unfairly. When we consider our sinfulness, we are reminded that God has not treated us as we should be treated. Instead, he has given us grace. Thank God for the grace that you do not deserve.

2. It is not necessary for us to "sell" the gospel to others through deception or distortion. The gospel can stand on its own. How are you sharing a diluted version of the gospel?

3. If you find yourself frustrated by the trials of life, memorize 2 Corinthians 4:8-9. The promise of that verse provides hope on dark days!

4. Reflecting on God's provision in the past provides strength for perseverance in the future! Reflect on the ways that God has blessed your family, not only your immediate family but your ancestors. Thank God for His past and future blessings.

JOB 37:1-39:30 2 CORINTHIANS 4:13-5:10 PSALM 44:9-26 PROVERBS 22:13	AUG **31**

Application:

1. Job's questions are answered by questions from God. Imbedded in God's questions are answers to Job's pleas. With his questions, God is revealing to Job and to us that He is the only one with the right to ask questions and that He is the only one capable of answering all questions. What questions would God ask of you today?

2. Take a few moments today to reflect on God's splendor revealed in creation. Praise Him for His creation and His creative power.

3. Grace received should increase the level of thanksgiving in your life. What are you thankful for today?

4. If you find yourself frustrated with the daily grind, don't worry, you are not home yet! Look ahead to the "eternal glory" promised in Christ. Thank God today that the body you tote around is only temporary.

_____

_____

_____

_____

_____

SEPTEMBER

JOB 40:1-42:17 2 CORINTHIANS 5:11-21 PSALM 45:1-17 PROVERBS 22:14	SEP 1

Application:

1. Job discovers that the glory of God silences the questions of man. Meditate on the majesty of God today.
2. Job had heard of God, but through this ordeal he saw God. (Job 42:5) If you find yourself struggling today, please press on. Keep reaching out to God. Don't give up. Sometimes we see God most clearly in the chaos of our lives.
3. Are you compelled by Christ's love to share God's grace? If not, what holds you back?
4. How has Christ transformed you into a new creation?
5. What type of ambassador for Christ are you?

| ECCLESIASTES 1:1-3:22
2 CORINTHIANS 6:1-13
PSALM 46:1-11
PROVERBS 22:15 | SEP
2 |

Application:

1. Solomon comments on the futility of earthly pursuits. When do you feel that your earthly pursuits are futile?
2. How do you seek pleasures in place of God?
3. How do you place your work over and above your relationship with God?
4. While Paul labored for the Corinthians, in print and in prayer, they seemed to turn a cold shoulder to the disciple. Are you honoring the ministers who labor for you? How can you show honor to those who minister to you?
5. If you are having trouble with fear and doubts, memorize Psalm 46:1-2.

_____

_____

_____

_____

_____

_____

| ECCLESIASTES 4:1-6:12
2 CORINTHIANS 6:14-7:7
PSALM 47:1-9
PROVERBS 22:16 | SEP
3 |

Application:

1. How are you striving for achievement and advancement to the detriment of your walk with God?
2. Who are the people in your life that support you? If you can readily think of those people, thank God. If not, ask God to provide strong, Christian friends.
3. Are you in partnership with unbelievers? Marital partnership, business partnership, etc.? How do these partnerships hinder your walk with God?
4. What is contaminating you spiritually?
5. Do you only give to those who can give more back to you?

_____

_____

_____

_____

_____

_____

_____

_____

ECCLESIASTES 7:1-9:18 2 CORINTHIANS 7:8-16 PSALM 48:1-14 PROVERBS 22:17-19	SEP **4**

Application:

1. Solomon warns against the practice of longing for the "good old days." When tempted to linger too long on memory lane, remind yourself that God is in control of the past, the present, and the future.

2. Life is brief. How does this knowledge impact the way you live your life?

3. Do you understand the difference between Godly sorrow and worldly sorrow? Worldly sorrow is inspired by Satan and drowns us in guilt. Godly sorrow is inspired by God and leads us to confession, repentance, and restored relationship. Which type of sorrow is at work in your life?

4. It is wise to memorize God's Word so that the Spirit of God can bring the Word of God to our mind. (Before you pretend that you cannot memorize Scripture, make a list of all the things you have memorized: phone numbers, baseball statistics, names, addresses, etc. You can memorize the things that are important to you!) Select a verse to memorize today.

_____

_____

_____

_____

ECCLESIASTES 10:1-12:14 2 CORINTHIANS 8:1-15 PSALM 49:1-20 PROVERBS 22:20-21	SEP 5

Application:

1. Don't postpone your walk with God. Many presume that they can "get right with God" at a later date. The later date is always on the horizon and rarely ever arrives. What are you postponing in your walk with God?

2. We are inundated with information, but the Bible still offers the best wisdom for living! What other voices compete with the voice of God in your life?

3. God will judge every deed. He sees the unseen in our lives, even our motivations. How will your deeds be judged?

4. Paul commends the churches in Macedonia for giving out of their poverty. While economic times force us to tighten our belts, remember that the needs of the hurting are ever before us! How can you help the hurting in your community?

SONG OF SONGS 1:1-4:16 2 CORINTHIANS 8:16-24 PSALM 50:1-23 PROVERBS 22:22-23	SEP 6

Application:

1. In Song of Solomon, the Bible celebrates the bond of love between husband and wife. The Bible does not gloss over this earthly relationship but celebrates it. As you read of the Lover and the Beloved, if you are married, thank God for the relationship God gives you with your spouse.

2. "...Do not arouse or awaken love until it so desires." (Song of Solomon 3:5) There is a proper time and place for the relationship described in Song of Solomon. The flames of passion that warm within marital relationship will scald outside it. When are you tempted to fan the flames of passion outside the bonds of marriage?

3. Paul indicates that he and the individuals with him on the missionary journey are striving to do the right thing in God's eyes and in the eyes of the Corinthians. When are you tempted to reverse the order of that priority list and concern yourself with the opinion of man before the opinion of God?

4. Paul speaks with great affinity of Titus and the other laborers that he sends to Corinth. They work with Paul for the sake of the gospel. Too many contemporary churchgoers see themselves as consumers rather than contributors. Are you a fellow servant with the teachers and ministers at your church or are you waiting to be served? How should you adjust your attitude and expectations?

| SONG OF SONGS 5:1-8:14
2 CORINTHIANS 9:1-15
PSALM 51:1-19
PROVERBS 22:24-25 | SEP
7 |

Application:

1. While the compliments recorded in Song of Solomon seem unusual to us, (eyes like doves and teeth like a flock of sheep), they remind us that we should provide verbal compliments to the ones we love. Don't try the sheep-teeth comparison, it won't translate well, but do think of something you can affirm in your spouse today.
2. How is your generosity?
3. Too many individuals claim Christ as Savior but deny Him as Lord through disobedience. How does obedience accompany your confession of Christ?
4. What sins do you need to confess before God today? Follow David's example of confession and experience the restored joy of salvation.

ISAIAH 1:1-2:22	SEP
2 CORINTHIANS 10:1-18	
PSALM 52:1-9	8
PROVERBS 22:26-27	

Application:

1. Isaiah condemns the people for piling up offerings while living in disobedience. How do you attempt to mask your sin? (Church attendance, giving, etc.)?

2. While we readily accept the fact that God will turn our scarlet sin to snow, do we acknowledge that grace requires surrender and obedience? What areas of your life are you hesitant to surrender to God?

3. Paul's comments reveal that people in the church of Corinth didn't like Paul's ministry style. It is a sobering reminder to us that when we become ministerial critics we can even find fault with the Apostle Paul. Are you currently on a fault-finding mission? Repent, and ask God to help you shift roles, from critic to supporter.

4. Are you allowing debt to destroy your life? Seek help from the Lord. Ask Him to help you stop spending beyond your means.

ISAIAH 3:1-5:30	SEP
2 CORINTHIANS 11:1-15	
PSALM 53:1-6	9
PROVERBS 22:28-29	

Application:

1. The women of Israel had replaced the jewels of heaven with the gems of the earth. (Isaiah 3:18-23) What can you do to transfer your focus from the jewelry and accessories of this world to the crown reserved for you in heaven?

2. Isaiah introduces the idea that God will preserve a remnant of His people. While Israel had widely abandoned God during Isaiah's era, God preserved a few as a righteous remnant. No matter how bad things seem today, God still has a remnant. Thank God, that He preserves His people.

3. One of the complaints against Paul was that his speaking did not measure up to the Corinthian standards. Do you place more value on a preacher's delivery or his heart? Ask God to help you see and value the heart of the minister more than their speaking ability.

4. Paul rebuked the Corinthians in love! Sometimes the most pointed and necessary rebukes come from the ones who love us. Who needs to receive a rebuke in love from you?

5. Are you skilled in your occupation? Remember, everything we do should be done to glorify God. What can you do to glorify God by improving your work skills?

_____

_____

_____

| ISAIAH 6:1-7:25
2 CORINTHIANS 11:16-33
PSALM 54:1-7
PROVERBS 23:1-3 | SEP
10 |

Application:

1. The Holiness of God drives Isaiah to his knees. God's Holiness should have the same impact on us. Take a few moments to meditate on the song of the seraphim, "Holy, holy, holy is the Lord Almighty; the whole earth is full of his glory." (Isaiah 6:3)

2. God still seeks those who are willing to answer His call. What is God calling you to do?

3. God's instructions to Isaiah remind us that just because we answer God's call, we are not guaranteed results. If you are growing weary in obedience, ask God to strengthen your resolve.

4. How can you boast in your weaknesses?

5. David notes that God is the one who sustains him. (Psalm 54:4) How can God sustain you today?

ISAIAH 8:1-9:21	SEP
2 CORINTHIANS 12:1-10	
PSALM 55:1-23	**11**
PROVERBS 23:4-5	

Application:

1. God warns against listening to the voice of the people. Isaiah is reminded to fear God first and foremost. How do your actions reveal a fear of God?

2. Isaiah 9:6 provides a prophetic prediction of Christ. Take a few moments to meditate on each of the names ascribed to Jesus. How is He the Wonderful Counselor, Mighty God, Everlasting Father, and Prince of Peace in your life?

3. God did not remove Paul's "thorn in the flesh." Sometimes the struggles of life are a part of God's plan. How is God using trials and difficulties to shape your life today?

4. When you face difficulties, remember the message God provided Paul, "My grace is sufficient for you, for my power is made perfect in weakness." (2 Corinthians 12:9) Work on committing this verse to memory.

5. How much time and energy are you investing in the pursuit of riches? Is it worth it?

_____

_____

_____

_____

ISAIAH 10:1-11:16	SEP
2 CORINTHIANS 12:11-21	
PSALM 56:1-13	**12**
PROVERBS 23:6-8	

Application:

1. God occasionally used pagan kings to punish His chosen people. When have you seen the ungodly used to bring about the purposes of God?

2. Amidst the message of judgment, God sprinkles the message of hope. Judgment is coming but so is deliverance. God's judgment must always be viewed in light of God's deliverance. When have you experienced God's judgment? When have you experienced His deliverance?

3. Isaiah prophecies of a day when the wolf and lamb will live in harmony. (Isaiah 11:6) This promise of a new world order will occur when Christ again reigns on the earth. Meditate on what this peaceful state will be like. Thank God for his promises.

4. What is the state of your church? Do quarreling, anger, jealousy, factions and slander exist? What are you doing to stop these forces?

5. What fears do you need to take to God? (Psalm 56:3)

ISAIAH 12:1-14:32 2 CORINTHIANS 13:1-14 PSALM 57:1-11 PROVERBS 23:9-11	**SEP** **13**

Application:

1. The people of God celebrate salvation by giving thanks to the Lord and making known among the nations what He has done. Share what God has done in your life with at least one person today.

2. Israel desired to see the "Day of the Lord." They did not recognize that on the Day of the Lord God intended to judge His people. Are you waiting for God to judge others? What if He judged you with the same measure you expect for others?

3. God used Babylon to judge Israel, and then God judged Babylon. While the unrighteous might appear to prosper, God's justice will ultimately prevail. When have you seen the unrighteous succumb to God's judgment?

4. "Examine yourselves to see whether you are in the faith;" (2 Corinthians 13:5) Take a few moments to examine yourself. Don't succumb to the temptation of assumption.

5. Paul's expectations are lofty. He instructs the Corinthians to aim for perfection. We cannot accept mediocrity in our Christian journey. How have you lowered your expectations to conform to the world?

_____

_____

_____

ISAIAH 15:1-18:7	SEP
GALATIANS 1:1-24	
PSALM 58:1-11	14
PROVERBS 23:12	

Application:

1. The people of Israel were perplexed by the ever-changing political scene around them. They wondered if God was in control. Isaiah relays the hopeful message, God is in control. In chaotic times, the people of God can trust that God is in control. Ask God to help you trust Him in the chaos of world politics.

2. If you believe in Christ, you have been rescued from the sins of this evil age. Spend some time thanking your rescuer.

3. What gospel do you follow? False teachers misled the Galatians with a false gospel; a gospel based on good-works and righteousness attained by action. Does your gospel match the Good News of the Bible?

4. What tempts you to abandon the Gospel of Christ?

ISAIAH 19:1-21:17 GALATIANS 2:1-16 PSALM 59:1-17 PROVERBS 23:13-14	SEP 15

Application:

1. The Egyptians, like others in the times of Isaiah, trusted in their leaders, their government and their military might. God warns that national identity will not overcome his plans. What tempts you to believe the lie that your ultimate security is found in your country?

2. Paul describes a moment when he was forced to confront Peter's hypocrisy. Is God calling you to confront sin in the life of a believer? Is so, learn from Paul's example. Paul spoke to Peter face to face about the issue. Don't lob anonymous attacks at other Christians; go speak to them face to face. Also, be willing to accept the rebuke of the saint who points out the error of your ways!

3. In Psalm 59, David pleads with God for deliverance. How are you in need of deliverance today?

4. Parents, you are given the responsibility of disciplining your children. If you do not provide your children with boundaries, they will drift listlessly through life like a ship with no sails. Help your children discover the proper limits in life. Ask God to help you provide proper discipline.

ISAIAH 22:1-24:23 GALATIANS 2:17-3:9 PSALM 60:1-12 PROVERBS 23:15-16	SEP **16**

Application:

1. Isaiah describes Israel's desperate attempts at defending the city of Jerusalem. While the people work feverishly, they fail to call on God. When have you attempted to fix things on your own? What can you learn from those situations?

2. As you watch the news today, thank God that He is not dependent on the rulers of the nations.

3. Are you constantly crucifying your old nature in order that Christ might live in you? This process is perpetual. Don't allow the old nature to maintain a foothold in the new life that God has planned for you. Ask God to reveal the works of the old nature that need to be removed from your life.

4. Salvation cannot be attained through good works. No amount of Bible reading or church attendance can attain salvation. When do you find yourself trying to earn God's salvation?

ISAIAH 25:1-28:13 GALATIANS 3:10-22 PSALM 61:1-8 PROVERBS 23:17-18	SEP 17

Application:

1. Isaiah offers a hopeful glimpse into the fulfillment of God's plan. The image of God removing tears and disgrace brings hope as we persevere in our faith. Take a few moments to meditate on the day of Christ's return.

2. Ask God to lead you on the straight path of obedience. (Isaiah 26:7-8)

3. If you have been a Christian for many years, you are susceptible to a dangerous lie. Satan wants you to believe that you are a good person and after attending church for a few years and changing a few behaviors it is easy to believe that myth. The wise Christian reflects often on their sinfulness. They recognize the depravity of sin and the inability of man to earn God's favor. Take a few moments today to reflect on your sinfulness and God's gift of grace.

4. Sin always looks appealing. Where are you tempted to exchange your future hope for temporary joy?

_____

_____

_____

_____

_____

| ISAIAH 28:14-30:11
GALATIANS 3:23-4:31
PSALM 62:1-12
PROVERBS 23:19-21 | SEP
18 |

Application:

1. Several New Testament writer's reference the cornerstone alluded to by Isaiah. (Isaiah 28:16) Christ is the cornerstone who provides a sure foundation. If you have placed your trust in Him, you will never be dismayed. Thank God for providing his cornerstone and pledge to make Christ the cornerstone of your life.

2. Israel was rebuked because their words and actions did not match. Do your words and actions match? How can you correct those areas where the words don't match the actions?

3. You are a child of God. How does that knowledge change your view of God, your life, and the world? (Galatians 3:26)

4. What does it mean for you to be "clothed" in Christ? (Galatians 3:27)

5. The teachers who sought to mislead the Galatians were zealous. Paul reminds that zeal is not an indicator of Truth. People can be passionately wrong. Where are you tempted to confuse fireworks for heat-producing flames?

_____

_____

_____

| ISAIAH 30:12-33:9
GALATIANS 5:1-12
PSALM 63:1-11
PROVERBS 23:22 | SEP
19 |

Application:

1. How are you resting in God? (Isaiah 30:15)
2. Idols always obstruct your relationship with God. Toss them out and embrace the True God! What idols need to be removed from your life?
3. Do not accept the yoke of legalism in your life. God has provided freedom in Christ. Legalism mocks Christ's sacrifice and enslaves the free. Where does legalism encroach on your faith?
4. How does your faith express itself through love?
5. Remember, we are called to honor our parents regardless of our age. What can you do today to honor your parents?

ISAIAH 33:10-36:22	SEP
GALATIANS 5:13-26	
PSALM 64:1-10	**20**
PROVERBS 23:23	

Application:

1. Isaiah contrasts those who are righteous with those who occupy positions of prominence. The righteous will "dwell on the heights" while the prestigious will disappear. (Isaiah 33:16) What are you doing that seeks prestige? What are you doing that seeks righteousness?

2. Isaiah predicts that water will gush forth in the wilderness. (Isaiah 35:6) Years after Isaiah, Jesus came to the earth offering Living Water. How has Living Water impacted your life?

3. Hezekiah was faced with insurmountable odds. You will see his response in tomorrow's reading. How do you handle insurmountable odds? What is your natural reaction?

4. Paul warned the Galatian church against biting and devouring one another. When have you experienced pain inflicted by other believers? When have you inflicted pain?

5. Look closely at the acts of the sinful nature. Check yourself against that list.

6. Where do you see evidence of the fruit of the Spirit in your life?

_____

_____

_____

| ISAIAH 37:1-38:22
GALATIANS 6:1-18
PSALM 65:1-13
PROVERBS 23:24 | SEP
21 |

Application:

1. Hezekiah sought God in the midst of his daunting situation. Do you have insurmountable issues to take to the All-Powerful God?

2. Ask God to help you be more concerned when He is insulted than when you are insulted?

3. Do you believe that God can provide victory over your enemies? Trust him for the victory today.

4. Christians are called to a ministry of burden sharing. This involves carrying the burdens of others. It also entails allowing others to carry your burdens. How are you at the ministry of burden sharing?

5. In what righteous actions are you becoming weary? Ask God for strength to persevere!

ISAIAH 39:1-41:16 EPHESIANS 1:1-23 PSALM 66:1-20 PROVERBS 23:25-28	SEP **22**

Application:

1. Hezekiah is punished for his pride. When do you show off your possessions and take credit for what you have accumulated?

2. Are you overwhelmed? Don't give up hope! God promises to renew the strength of those who continue to trust in Him. (Isaiah 40:31) Confess your feelings of being overwhelmed and trust God's promise of renewal.

3. Thank God for the spiritual blessings you have received.

4. Who are you thankful for today?

5. Pray that God will open the eyes of your heart that you might know the hope to which you have been called. (Ephesians 1:18)

ISAIAH 41:17-43:13	SEP
EPHESIANS 2:1-22	
PSALM 67:1-7	23
PROVERBS 23:29-35	

Application:

1. The Israelites Isaiah addressed ignored God's warnings. How might God be warning you?

2. God promises His protective presence to those who follow Him. Are you struggling through fiery trials? Trust God's promised presence.

3. How are you attempting to earn salvation through your works? Remember, salvation is by grace alone. (Ephesians 2:8-9)

4. Thank God that He gives grace freely.

5. Once you have experienced God's grace, you should do good works. (Ephesians 2:10) Good works do not earn salvation but they bear testimony of salvation. Ask God to help you keep the proper perspective on this crucial issue.

6. Is Jesus the cornerstone of your church? What are you doing to make Him the cornerstone?

ISAIAH 43:14-45:10 EPHESIANS 3:1-21 PSALM 68:1-18 PROVERBS 24:1-2	SEP **24**

Application:

1. Reflect on your sin for a few moments. Now praise God that He has blotted out your sin through the blood of Christ. (Isaiah 43:25)

2. What are you worshipping? Are you worshipping things you have made with your own hands? (Your career, your marriage, your wealth, etc.?)

3. What do you learn from the image of the clay talking back to the potter? (Isaiah 45:9)

4. How many times does Paul speak of the mystery of Christ? What is your responsibility in revealing this mystery?

5. Pray that God would give you the power to grasp and appreciate the expanse of His love that surpasses all understanding. (Ephesians 3:18-19)

6. Do you respect and seek to imitate individuals whose values differ from your own? Make a list of individuals in your life that you can imitate who seek to honor God. Seek to follow their Godly example.

| ISAIAH 45:11-48:11
EPHESIANS 4:1-16
PSALM 68:19-35
PROVERBS 24:3-4 | SEP
25 |

Application:

1. God was faithful to Israel through all of her disobedience. How does that reassure you of God's love?

2. God led Israel through the refining fire of conquest and exile because He loved them. How is God leading you through difficulties in order to draw you back to Him?

3. What does it mean "to live a life worthy of the calling" of God? (Ephesians 4:1)

4. How does the reminder that we serve one God and Father impact your view of other Christians and fellow church members?

5. Do you have difficulty speaking the truth in love? Ask God to help you season your speech with love.

ISAIAH 48:12-50:11 EPHESIANS 4:17-32 PSALM 69:1-18 PROVERBS 24:5-6	SEP **26**

Application:

1. Spend a few minutes meditating on the creative capacity of God.

2. Isaiah reports that the promised Messiah would be a light to all nations. (Isaiah 49:6) What are you doing to spread the light beyond your community?

3. How is your life different today than it was before you met Christ? How is it different today than it was last year?

4. Has anger found a foothold in your life? Seek God's power to overcome anger.

5. How can you use your tongue to build up other believers?

_____

_____

_____

_____

_____

_____

_____

ISAIAH 51:1-53:12	SEP
EPHESIANS 5:1-33	
PSALM 69:19-36	**27**
PROVERBS 24:7	

Application:

1. Do not fear the words of enemies or economists; fear God. Ask God to give you the faith to fear Him above all else.

2. Meditate on the reality that your sins crushed Christ. (Isaiah 53:5) Then, offer prayers of thanksgiving for his sacrifice.

3. Are you imitating God? In what areas are you succeeding in this endeavor and in what areas are you failing?

4. How are you allowing a hint of sexual immorality in your life?

5. Husband, how does your love for your spouse reflect Christ's love for the church?

| ISAIAH 54:1-57:14
EPHESIANS 6:1-24
PSALM 70:1-5
PROVERBS 24:8 | SEP
28 |

Application:

1. How do the names Maker, Lord Almighty, and Redeemer inform your understanding of God?
2. In what areas are you settling for the scraps of the world rather than feasting on the food God provides? (Isaiah 55:2)
3. What causes you to question God's ways? Pray that God will remind you of the impassable divide between His ways and yours.
4. What are you doing to honor your parents?
5. How does Paul's revelation that your battle is not against flesh and blood impact your view of the people around you? (Ephesians 6:12)
6. Meditate on the armor of God. Thank God for the protection His armor has already provided in the past and will provide in the future.

ISAIAH 57:15-59:21 PHILIPPIANS 1:1-26 PSALM 71:1-24 PROVERBS 24:9-10	SEP **29**

Application:

1. Do you recognize the depravity of your own sin? God offers mercy to those who recognize their sin. Meditate on the depths of your sin.

2. Israel practiced public religion for the purpose of manipulating God. What do you do for the purpose of manipulating God?

3. We cannot expect God's response to our prayers when our lives are soaked with sin. Ask the Holy Spirit to reveal your unconfessed sins.

4. Are you frustrated by your lack of spiritual growth? Take heart with the reminder that God will complete the work that He has started. (Philippians 1:6)

5. "...to live is Christ and to die is gain." (Philippians 1:21) Does your life reflect this sentiment? If not, what needs to change?

ISAIAH 60:1-62:5 PHILIPPIANS 1:27-2:18 PSALM 72:1-20 PROVERBS 24:11-12	SEP **30**

Application:

1. The promises of Isaiah appear to coincide with the New Testament prediction that God will be the source of light in eternity. (Isaiah 60:1-3 & Revelation 22:5) Note that God's Holiness replaces the scalding sun. What does this tell you about God's holiness?

2. Israel awaits a time of judgment but God promises a future of renewal. Are you currently experiencing trials? Pray that God will remind you that relief is on the horizon.

3. What should you change in order to live in a manner worthy of the gospel? (Philippians 1:27)

4. In what areas do you tend to operate out of selfish ambition? (Philippians 2:3) Follow the example of Christ and place others ahead of yourself.

5. At home or at church, do you complain and argue? (Philippians 2:14) These seemingly insignificant actions can create chaos in the church and home.

_____

_____

_____

_____

_____

WHAT NOW?

OCTOBER

ISAIAH 62:6-65:25 PHILIPPIANS 2:19-3:3 PSALM 73:1-28 PROVERBS 24:13-14	OCT **1**

Application:

1. Isaiah promises Israel that they "will be called Sought After" and "the City No Longer Deserted." (Isaiah 62:12) Have you ever considered that God is seeking you? Praise God for seeking you.

2. Where do you resist the work of the Potter in your life? (Isaiah 64:8)

3. Paul affirms Timothy's service to the gospel. Who could you encourage today? Like Timothy, someone in your sphere of influence needs to know that they are appreciated.

4. Paul instructs the believers in Philippi to rejoice. He is not advising the Philippians to pretend that trials do not exist. He is encouraging them to find joy in Christ in spite of the external trials. Find joy in the Lord today.

ISAIAH 66:1-24 PHILIPPIANS 3:4-21 PSALM 74:1-23 PROVERBS 24:15-16	OCT **2**

Application:

1. Imagine the scene described in Isaiah 66:1. Allow that image to inform your worship today.

2. Paul recognized that all his religious efforts were worthless. Make a list of all your religious efforts apart from Christ. After you write each item on the list, strike through it to remind you that the religious efforts are worthless.

3. Ask God to increase your desire to "know Christ and the power of his resurrection." (Philippians 3:10)

4. What does Paul mean when he says he wants to share in Christ's suffering? (Philippians 3:10)

5. How is your past prohibiting you from pressing toward the goal of Christ?

6. How do your actions reflect that you are a citizen of heaven? (Philippians 3:20)

_____

_____

_____

_____

_____

JEREMIAH 1:1-2:30	OCT
PHILIPPIANS 4:1-23	
PSALM 75:1-10	3
PROVERBS 24:17-20	

Application:

1. Like Jeremiah, God knew you before you were born and set you apart for a special purpose. How does God want to use you to advance His kingdom?

2. If God calls you to a task, He has provided the skills to complete the task. How are you currently resisting God's call?

3. What can you do to maintain your reverence and respect for God?

4. A feud between Euodia and Syntyche threatened the church in Philippi. (Philippians 4:2) Are you nursing a feud that threatens your church? Resolve the dispute so that your church can move forward.

5. Prayer eradicates anxiety. Don't allow worries to rob you of mental and emotional health. (Philippians 4:6) Make a list of your concerns. Commit each to God individually.

6. Evaluate your thoughts according to the admonition in Philippians 4:8.

JEREMIAH 2:31-4:18 COLOSSIANS 1:1-17 PSALM 76:1-12 PROVERBS 24:21-22	OCT **4**

Application:

1. The prophet compares Israel to a prostitute, peddling her affections to the highest bidder. How is your pursuit of false gods equivalent to spiritual adultery?

2. Israel refused to take an introspective look at their sinful ways. Take a hard look at your actions in light of God's Holiness? It might not be pleasant but it will be profitable.

3. Who can you pray for today that needs to be filled with the knowledge of God's will?

4. Is your life bearing the fruit of the gospel? If not, what changes need to be made to facilitate better fruit production?

5. What does Jesus reveal to you about God?

6. The reconciliation predicted in Isaiah is available through Christ. Have you been reconciled to God through His Son? If you have, thank Him for the reconciling gift of Christ.

_____

_____

_____

_____

_____

JEREMIAH 4:19-6:15 COLOSSIANS 1:18-2:7 PSALM 77:1-20 PROVERBS 24:23-25	OCT **5**

Application:

1. Israel refused to acknowledge God's rebuke. How are you ignoring the warning signs of God in your life?
2. In what ways are you tempted to take God for granted? (His grace? His provision? etc.)
3. Paul labored to teach everyone that they might be perfect in Christ. (Colossians 1:28) How are you striving for perfection in Christ?
4. Notice that Paul labored with the energy of Christ. (Colossians 1:29) How can you utilize the energy of Christ in your labors?
5. Does thankfulness overflow in your life? How can you express your gratitude to God?

| JEREMIAH 6:16-8:7
COLOSSIANS 2:8-23
PSALM 78:1-31
PROVERBS 24:26 | OCT
6 |

Application:

1. Have you lost the ability to blush at sin? Ask God to help you see sin from His holy perspective.

2. Israel worshipped God as one of many options. Worship was a ritual. How does your worship resemble a ritual? How does your worship resemble a relationship?

3. Paul warns the Colossians to guard against human traditions and worldly principles creeping into their faith. (Colossians 2:8) We should diligently protect against the same enemies. Think through your faith practices. Are they grounded in Scripture? If not, are they grounded in human tradition?

4. Paul eloquently describes Christ's triumph on the cross which allowed us to move from death in sin to life in Christ. (Colossians 2:13-15) Take a few minutes to contemplate the eternal significance of these verses.

_____

_____

_____

_____

_____

JEREMIAH 8:8-9:26 COLOSSIANS 3:1-17 PSALM 78:32-55 PROVERBS 24:27	OCT **7**

Application:

1. The scribes handled the word of God falsely. (Jeremiah 8:8) This led the nation to sin. Pray that those who teach you will handle God's Word accurately. Also pray that you will interpret God's Word accurately.

2. Jeremiah has been called the weeping prophet. He wept over the sins of his people. Ask God to help you mourn the sins of the Christian church today.

3. How do you "Set your minds on things above"? (Colossians 3:2)

4. What sinful habits need to be put to death in your life?

5. It is not enough to get rid of sinful habits; Christ compels us to cloth ourselves with compassion, kindness, humility, gentleness and patience. Meditate on each of these characteristics. How is God calling you to grow in each of these attributes?

| JEREMIAH 10:1-11:23
COLOSSIANS 3:18-4:18
PSALM 78:56-72
PROVERBS 24:28-29 | OCT
8 |

Application:

1. What man-made object receives your worship?

2. Jeremiah's obedience makes him a target of those who are in rebellion against God. When have you been targeted for your obedience?

3. Would your employer, neighbor or family member say that you work at everything as if you were working for the Lord? Why or why not? (Colossians 3:23-24)

4. Paul requested prayer for his ministry. (Colossians 4:3-4) Who needs your prayer support today?

5. Ask God to fill your conversations with grace.

6. Who are you seeking to repay with evil? Instead of carrying out revenge, ask God to give you the strength to forgive that individual so that you can move on in your faith.

_____

_____

_____

_____

_____

_____

JEREMIAH 12:1-14:10 1 THESSALONIANS 1:1-2:8 PSALM 79:1-13 PROVERBS 24:30-34	OCT 9

Application:

1. In what areas does your stubborn pride make you useless to God?

2. Do you, like Israel, frequently wander from God's path? What changes do you need to make in your life to still your wandering soul?

3. Are you a model for other believers? Why or why not? (1 Thessalonians 1:7)

4. When we share the gospel we also share our lives. (1 Thessalonians 2:8) How can you invest your life in someone today who needs the gospel of Jesus?

5. When you request God's intervention, do you base your request on your needs or God's glory? Our motivation in everything should be to glorify God! (Psalm 79:9)

JEREMIAH 14:11-16:15	OCT
1 THESSALONIANS 2:9-3:13	
PSALM 80:1-19	**10**
PROVERBS 25:1-5	

Application:

1. False prophets tell people what they want to hear. Commit to test the messages of God's messengers. Make sure that you base your test on God's Word and not man's opinions.

2. The purpose of God's punishment is restoration. God wants to restore people to right relationship with Him. How is God disciplining you in an effort to restore your relationship with Him? Thank God for His discipline.

3. Paul encouraged, comforted and urged the Thessalonians to "live lives worthy of God." (1Thessalonians 2:12) Who do you know that needs to be encouraged, comforted, and urged to live a life worthy of God?

4. Pray that God would allow your love for Him to overflow into the lives of others.

_____

_____

_____

_____

_____

_____

JEREMIAH 16:16-18:23 1 THESSALONIANS 4:1-5:3 PSALM 81:1-16 PROVERBS 25:6-8	OCT **11**

Application:

1. God sees sin. Your sin is as obvious to God as the sin of Israel denounced by Jeremiah. What do you need to confess that God already knows?

2. When has your heart deceived you? When has your heart led you to sin? What precautions can you take to avoid similar pitfalls?

3. How is your life moldable in God's hands?

4. Ask God to help you control your own body "in a way that is holy and honorable." (1 Thessalonians 4:4)

5. Make a list of those you look forward to seeing when the trumpet call of God sounds. (Is Jesus at the top of your list?)

_____

_____

_____

_____

_____

_____

_____

JEREMIAH 19:1-21:14	OCT
1 THESSALONIANS 5:4-28	
PSALM 82:1-8	**12**
PROVERBS 25:9-10	

Application:

1. Jeremiah was abused for revealing Truth. When does fear prohibit you from sharing Truth?

2. King Zedekiah presumed that God would work on Israel's behalf. How do you presume on God?

3. What is God doing in the world around you? Where is He inviting you to join Him?

4. When was the last time you showed appreciation to those in spiritual authority? Send your pastor, minister, or small group leader a card expressing how important they are to you.

5. Thank God for five things.

JEREMIAH 22:1-23:20 2 THESSALONIANS 1:1-12 PSALM 83:1-18 PROVERBS 25:11-14	OCT 13

Application:

1. Jeremiah promises judgment on Israel when they fail to defend the oppressed. Who can you defend today?

2. While Jeremiah provided accurate messages from God, other false prophets distorted God's Word. False prophets still twist God's Word. How do you recognize that a message deviates from God's word?

3. The church in Thessalonica modeled perseverance in persecution. When you struggle, pray that God will grant you the strength to persevere with faithfulness.

4. Pray for a fellow believer today the way Paul prayed in 2 Thessalonians 1:11. Pray that God would count them worthy of His calling and that by His power He may fulfill every good purpose they undertake and every act prompted by their faith.

5. Pray that God will protect your tongue so that you will offer only the choicest of words. (Proverbs 25:11)

JEREMIAH 23:21-25:38	OCT
2 THESSALONIANS 2:1-17	
PSALM 84:1-12	**14**
PROVERBS 25:15	

Application:

1. God is not limited by space or time. (Jeremiah 23:23-24) Ponder this incredible truth today. How does this impact your understanding of God?

2. With the image of the figs, God reveals to Jeremiah that the exiles in Babylon actually have greater hope than the ones left in Israel. (Jeremiah 24) This should remind us that circumstances never explain God's actions with absolute accuracy. What circumstances in your life are proving difficult to discern? Ask for God's wisdom concerning those issues.

3. How do you see examples of Satan's activity in the world?

4. If, like Paul, you are thankful for certain individuals, then make sure that you tell them how much you appreciate them. (2 Thessalonians 2:13)

5. Who needs a word of "eternal encouragement" today? (2 Thessalonians 2:16)

JEREMIAH 26:1-27:22 2 THESSALONIANS 3:1-18 PSALM 85:1-13 PROVERBS 25:16	OCT 15

Application:

1. Truth is rarely popular. How can you stand for Truth?
2. Some pastors and teachers tell you what you want to hear while others tell you what you need to hear? Which do you prefer? Which is more profitable?
3. How can you pray consistently and specifically for the spread of the gospel? (2 Thessalonians 3:18)
4. How do you balance between shaming the disobedient and warning them like a brother? (2 Thessalonians 3:14-15)
5. If you have a tendency to over-indulge, ask God to give you restraint. (Proverbs 25:16)

JEREMIAH 28:1-29:32 1 TIMOTHY 1:1-20 PSALM 86:1-17 PROVERBS 25:17	OCT **16**

Application:

1. Jeremiah's letter to the exiles encouraged them to continue faithful living in exile. In the face of turmoil, Israel was encouraged to keep the faith. How does turmoil threaten to draw you away from your faith? Continue to trust God's plan and purpose.

2. God promises the exiles that they will find Him when they seek Him with all their heart. (Jeremiah 29:13) How would you describe the way that you are currently seeking God?

3. What issues promote controversy and conflict in the church? What issues promote health and maturity? (1 Timothy 1:4)

4. God used Paul's sinful past as a testimony to His transforming grace. (1 Timothy 1:16) How can God receive glory from your past?

5. God is forgiving and good. How does this revelation from Psalm 86:5 assist your understanding of God?

_____

_____

_____

_____

_____

JEREMIAH 30:1-31:26	OCT
1 TIMOTHY 2:1-15	
PSALM 87:1-7	**17**
PROVERBS 25:18-19	

Application:

1. God instructed Jeremiah to record all the words He had spoken. This record reminds us of God's providence and revelation. Thank God for preserving these events to strengthen your faith.

2. God promises the restoration of Israel. The restoration of this tiny nation foreshadows God's restoration of the world through Jesus. Pray that God will use you in the process of restoration.

3. Do you pray for the president? The governor? The mayor? While you might not agree with their politics, they can all use your prayers.

4. How did Jesus serve as a ransom for your sins? How can you show your appreciation to Him for that act?

5. Paul did not want women to draw attention to themselves in their dress. (1 Timothy 2:9-10) How do you draw attention to yourself and distract others from God?

_____

_____

_____

_____

_____

JEREMIAH 31:27-32:44	OCT
1 TIMOTHY 3:1-16	
PSALM 88:1-18	**18**
PROVERBS 25:20-22	

Application:

1. Through Jeremiah, God speaks of a New Covenant that is distinct from the Old Covenant. (Jeremiah 31:33) How is the New Covenant through Christ, different from the covenant with Israel?

2. Jeremiah purchased a piece of land in the midst of a siege. (Jeremiah 32:7) Although Judah was about to fall, the prophet trusted God's assurance that His people would one day repopulate the land. Do you find it difficult to trust God in times of despair? Even in the sieges of life, God is still on His throne!

3. God says that He will give the children of the New Covenant "singleness of heart and action." (Jeremiah 32:39) How do you display a singleness of heart toward God?

4. How do the requirements for church leadership apply to the leadership in your church?

5. How can you show kindness to an enemy today?

_____

_____

_____

_____

JEREMIAH 33:1-34:22 1 TIMOTHY 4:1-16 PSALM 89:1-13 PROVERBS 25:23-24	OCT 19

Application:

1. God instructs Israel to call to Him while in exile. (Jeremiah 33:3) God promises that He will reveal great things to those who call on Him. What do you expect when you call to God in prayer?

2. God's promises are as certain as the rising and setting of the sun. (Jeremiah 33:19-22) Watch the sun set today and thank God for the consistency of His promises.

3. The Israelites did not show grace and mercy to their Hebrew slaves as God had commanded. They failed to recognize the grace God gave them. How can the people around you see the grace that you've received?

4. Timothy was instructed to guard against false teaching. How do you protect against false teaching?

5. How is your speech, life, love, and faith an example to those around you? (1 Timothy 4:12)

_____

_____

_____

_____

_____

JEREMIAH 35:1-36:32	OCT
1 TIMOTHY 5:1-25	
PSALM 89:14-37	**20**
PROVERBS 25:25-27	

Application:

1. Jonadab son of Recab started a legacy of faith. What is your faith legacy?

2. Jehoiakim rejected God's commands by literally burning up the word of the Lord. Which areas of Scripture do you avoid because they make you uncomfortable?

3. How are you practicing your faith by caring for older family members?

4. What do people see in your life? Good deeds? Sinfulness?

5. How do you seek honor for yourself by tooting your own horn? (Proverbs 25:27)

JEREMIAH 37:1-38:28	OCT
1 TIMOTHY 6:1-21	
PSALM 89:38-52	**21**
PROVERBS 25:28	

Application:

1. The king ignored the word of God, yet still sought the Lord's favor. In what ways do you do the same?

2. If you are in a pit today, trust that God will send a rescuer. If you are not in a pit, go rescue someone who is!

3. Do you work for your boss as if you were working for Christ? If not, how can you adjust your work ethic and attitudes to better reflect Christ?

4. Ask God to cultivate contentment in your heart. (1 Timothy 6:6)

5. How can you flee from the temptations you face? (1 Timothy 6:11)

6. What treasures are you storing in heaven? (1 Timothy 6:19)

JEREMIAH 39:1-41:18 2 TIMOTHY 1:1-18 PSALM 90:1-91:16 PROVERBS 26:1-2	OCT **22**

Application:

1. On Israel's darkest day, Jeremiah is vindicated. Jeremiah is rewarded and recognized by Israel's enemies. If you are standing up under persecution, thank God that one day you will be vindicated.

2. After Israel fell, the remnant endured a tumultuous period of chaos. The absence of leadership often causes chaos. How can you be a calming influence during times of instability?

3. If you feel timid, ask God to increase your power, love, and self-discipline. (1 Timothy 1:7)

4. How are you at protecting that which God has entrusted to you?

5. What is required to dwell in the shelter of the Most High?

_____

_____

_____

_____

_____

_____

JEREMIAH 42:1-44:23	OCT
2 TIMOTHY 2:1-21	**23**
PSALM 92:1-93:5	
PROVERBS 26:3-5	

Application:

1. The Israelites trusted the protection of Egypt over God. Who or what are you trusting for your protection?
2. Israel offered sacrifices to the Queen of Heaven in spite of Jeremiah's warnings. What false god threatens your worship of God?
3. The gospel centers on the resurrection of Jesus Christ. How does your life center on Christ's resurrection?
4. What steps can you take to handle God's word better?
5. Godless chatter is an infection that kills the church. How are you spreading the infection?
6. Ask God to help you become an instrument for noble purposes.

JEREMIAH 44:24-47:7	OCT
2 TIMOTHY 2:22-3:17	
PSALM 94:1-23	**24**
PROVERBS 26:6-8	

Application:

1. Jeremiah is called the "weeping prophet." When you decry the evils of society, do you speak with tears?
2. Nationalistic allegiances melt before the power of God. In what ways do you trust government to do what only God can do?
3. Are you quarrelsome? There is a difference between standing for Truth and picking fights. How can you stand for Truth without being quarrelsome?
4. Thank God for the individuals who nurtured you in the faith. How can you honor them today?
5. Every page of Scripture contains the very breath of God. How does that impact the way you read and study the Bible? (2 Timothy 3:16)

JEREMIAH 48:1-49:22 2 TIMOTHY 4:1-22 PSALM 95:1-96:13 PROVERBS 26:9-12	OCT **25**

Application:

1. Moab is the object of God's rebuke. The nation was guilty of arrogance. How is your nation guilty of the same arrogance?

2. God promises judgment on Ammon and Edom as well. Nations that reject God might prosper for a period of time, but their sin does not escape the eyes of God. Pray for those living in countries that actively oppress Christians.

3. Paul commands Timothy to correct, rebuke and encourage. How do you accept correction and rebuke from your spiritual leaders?

4. Think about your life and your walk with Christ. Can you say, with Paul, that you have fought the good fight? If not, what is holding you back?

5. Do you find yourself repeating the same mistakes? Ask God for wisdom.

JEREMIAH 49:23-50:46 TITUS 1:1-16 PSALM 97:1-98:9 PROVERBS 26:13-16	OCT **26**

Application:

1. Though God used Babylon to punish Israel, God promises punishment on Babylon as well. If circumstances seem unfair, remember that God's justice will ultimately be fulfilled. Ask God to help you to trust His timing.

2. God provides a promise of restoration and forgiveness to exiled Israel. Think about the restoration that God has accomplished in your life. Praise Him for bringing you out of exile!

3. Who is attempting to deceive you and mislead you in your faith?

4. How do your actions support your claim to know God?

5. Read aloud the selection from Psalms today as a prayer of praise to God.

6. What excuses contribute to laziness in your life?

_____

_____

_____

_____

_____

JEREMIAH 51:1-53 TITUS 2:1-15 PSALM 99:1-9 PROVERBS 26:17	OCT **27**

Application:

1. What worthless idols clutter your life?
2. When Jeremiah proclaimed judgment on Babylon, the nation was a superpower. The Lord's judgment ultimately prevailed. Remember, God's power is far greater than any nation!
3. Paul provides guidelines for men and women both young and old. Evaluate yourself by the appropriate standards. How do you measure up?
4. Which worldly passions do you have difficulty saying "No" to?
5. How do you allow spiritual leaders to have authority in your life?
6. What can you do to avoid quarrels that don't concern you?

_____

_____

_____

_____

_____

_____

| JEREMIAH 51:54-52:34
TITUS 3:1-15
PSALM 100:1-5
PROVERBS 26:18-19 | OCT
28 |

Application:

1. The sinking scroll must have lifted the spirits of the Israelites in Babylon. (Jeremiah 51:64) Remember that whatever troubles you face today they are "light and momentary" (2 Corinthians 4:17). Just as God rescued Israel from exile, He will rescue you!

2. The description of people and property taken into exile is a sad reminder of the consequences of sin. What consequences do you risk by continuing in your sin?

3. When are you tempted to slander others?

4. How can you be more peaceable?

5. Would others describe you as humble? Why or why not? How can you display humility?

LAMENTATIONS 1:1-2:22	OCT
PHILEMON 1:1-25	
PSALM 101:1-8	**29**
PROVERBS 26:20	

Application:

1. The forlorn lament of Jeremiah reminds us of the emptiness of sin. Think about a time when you recognized the emptiness of sin. What are you engaged in today that will lead you to the same desperate emptiness?
2. Are you currently being punished by God for sin? Accept God's discipline as an expression of His love.
3. Paul makes a bold appeal on behalf of a slave, Onesimus. Who needs your bold voice today? Remember, your silence perpetuates injustice.
4. The Psalmist seeks to be blameless before God. How are you seeking to do the same?
5. How can you silence the gossip that takes place around you?

LAMENTATIONS 3:1-66	OCT
HEBREWS 1:1-14	
PSALM 102:1-28	**30**
PROVERBS 26:21-22	

Application:

1. Jeremiah faithfully followed God's instructions, yet the people refused to repent and receive God's judgment. Like Jeremiah, have you ever been upset by the reaction (or lack of reaction) of others? Jeremiah found hope in God's love even in the midst of despair.

2. If you are mourning today, remember that God's compassions are new every morning. Continue to cling to the Lord who will provide! In the midst of perpetual change it is encouraging to remember that God never changes. With whom can you share this word of hope today?

3. Just as God spoke through the burning bush He speaks through His Word. How does the knowledge that God has spoken to you impact your understanding of God? Of the Bible?

4. People often speak of guardian angels but as the author of Hebrews reveals, Jesus is greater than any angel. How does that influence your opinion of Jesus?

LAMENTATIONS 4:1–5:22	OCT
HEBREWS 2:1–18	
PSALM 103:1–22	31
PROVERBS 26:23	

Application:

1. The physical destruction of Israel mirrored their spiritual decay. Spend some time in prayer today for the spiritual state of your nation.

2. As you consider the complexity of God's Creation, recognize that God is mindful of and cares for man. How does that inform your understanding of God?

3. Jesus took on flesh and blood so that He could forgive you of your sins. Praise Jesus for His sacrifice!

4. How does it encourage you to know that Jesus was tempted as you are tempted?

5. God sees through your words to your heart. What is the correlation between your lips and your heart?

_____

_____

_____

_____

_____

_____

November

EZEKIEL 1:1–3:15 HEBREWS 3:1–19 PSALM 104:1–23 PROVERBS 26:24–26	NOV 1

Application:

1. Ezekiel falls facedown when he sees the glory of God. Allow yourself to be overwhelmed by God's presence today. Meditate on His character and power.

2. When do you refrain from sharing Truth because you know it will not be popular?

3. Sometimes the most difficult mission field is the one closest to home. Who do you have difficulty reaching because you are too close to them? Ask God to open a door so that you can reach them.

4. Who can you encourage today? Look for someone who is facing temptation, (temptation to doubt, temptation to give up hope, temptation to immorality), and give them an encouraging nudge.

5. How has your commitment for Christ changed from the time you started your walk of faith to now?

6. Ask God to protect you from the deceitful speech that surrounds you.

_____

_____

_____

_____

EZEKIEL 3:16-6:14 HEBREWS 4:1-16 PSALM 104:24-35 PROVERBS 26:27	NOV 2

Application:

1. Ezekiel is responsible for how he delivers the truth, not how the people respond to the truth. Are you carrying unnecessary guilt for those who have rejected Truth? Recognize that you cannot force someone into faith; they must make their own decision to follow.

2. Throughout Ezekiel's prophecies, God speaks of a remnant that He will retain. The remnant reveals God's mercy. While God had the right to destroy the nation entirely, He offered grace. Pray that God will have grace on your country.

3. The Israelites missed God's message because they forgot faith. How are you attempting to earn grace? Remember it can only be received through faith.

4. Are you allowing God's Word to penetrate your life or are you simply allowing the Word to skim the surface? How can you let the Word rearrange your life!

5. How do the temptations Christ endured and conquered encourage you to open up to Him in prayer?

6. Are you seeking revenge on someone? Have you ever considered that they have likely already forgotten the incident? Ask God to help you forgive and forget.

EZEKIEL 7:1-9:11 HEBREWS 5:1-14 PSALM 105:1-15 PROVERBS 26:28	NOV 3

Application:

1. Ask God to help you see sin as He sees sin.
2. How can you stand against things that are detestable to the Lord?
3. How do your prayers reflect humility and reverent submission?
4. How have you matured and grown in your faith? In what areas do you need to mature?
5. While flattery might advance you on the corporate ladder, it will not advance you in the kingdom. When do you use flattering language for personal gain? (Proverbs 26:28)

EZEKIEL 10:1-11:25 **HEBREWS 6:1-20** **PSALM 105:16-36** **PROVERBS 27:1-2**	**NOV** **4**

Application:

1. Is your heart divided? (Ezekiel 11:19) If so, ask God to perform a heart transplant! Seek an undivided heart for Him.
2. How have you matured beyond conversion? Ask God to help you strike out into the deep waters of faith.
3. In what areas of your life are you producing abundant crops? In what areas of your life are you producing thorns and thistles? (Hebrews 6:7-8)
4. How does God's faithfulness encourage you today?
5. In what ways do you "boast about tomorrow"? (Proverbs 27:1)

EZEKIEL 12:1-14:11	NOV
HEBREWS 7:1-17	
PSALM 105:37-45	**5**
PROVERBS 27:3	

Application:

1. Israel mistook God's delay for His absence. What is your attitude toward Christ's return?

2. The prophets of Israel are rebuked for giving a flimsy, false message that they coated in flowering words. Where are you tempted to believe flowery words, (white washed walls), and miss God's leadership? (Ezekiel 13:8-12)

3. While horoscopes might appear harmless, they actually divert our attention from God. How are you allowing horoscopes, psychics, and other pagan rituals to deceive you?

4. Reflect on how the priesthood of Jesus surpasses any Old Testament priest. Thank God that your priest is accessible and available.

EZEKIEL 14:12-16:41 HEBREWS 7:18-28 PSALM 106:1-12 PROVERBS 27:4-6	NOV **6**

Application:

1. The story of destitute Israel in Ezekiel 16 mirrors our story. Like Israel, we were helpless and hopeless. Do you remember your hopelessness without Christ? Take a few moments to reflect on God's grace.

2. Meditate on the way idolatry breaks the heart of God? Have you committed adultery with false idols?

3. The new covenant through Christ allows us to draw near to God. Are you staying distant from God in ritual or drawing near to God through relationship? How can you draw near Him?

4. How can Jesus endure temptation like us yet also be set apart from us? How do those two realities inform your faith?

5. Thank God today for His goodness and enduring love. (Psalm 106:1)

_____

_____

_____

_____

_____

EZEKIEL 16:42-17:24 HEBREWS 8:1-13 PSALM 106:13-31 PROVERBS 27:7-9	NOV **7**

Application:

1. Sodom was arrogant, overfed, and unconcerned. Does this description sound familiar to you? Could it be used to describe you? Pray that God will start a revival in you that will pour forth into others.

2. God atoned for your idolatry through the cross of Jesus Christ. We cannot fully appreciate the cross until we fully grasp the depths of our depravity. Thank God for overcoming your idolatry.

3. God is greater than any nation. He brings nations to power and allows them to fall. Pray for God's will to be accomplished through the nations of this world.

4. Isaiah, Jeremiah and Ezekiel have provided a solid foundation for understanding the new covenant described in Hebrews. How does the new covenant differ from the old covenant? How does the new covenant encourage you today?

EZEKIEL 18:1-19:14 **HEBREWS 9:1-10** **PSALM 106:32-48** **PROVERBS 27:10**	**NOV** **8**

Application:

1. Ezekiel clearly states that each individual is accountable for their own actions. How are you relying on the faith of your ancestors to save you? How are you using the sins of your ancestors to limit your own faith?

2. Do you delight in the destruction of the wicked? Ask God to tune your heart to match His heart concerning the wicked and disobedient.

3. Ask God to give you a new heart and new spirit. (Ezekiel 18:31)

4. What can you do to transform your faith from expressions of external religion to acts of internal devotion?

5. Who can you turn to in times of distress? Who can turn to you? (Proverbs 27:10)

_____

_____

_____

_____

_____

_____

EZEKIEL 20:1-49	NOV
HEBREWS 9:11-28	
PSALM 107:1-43	9
PROVERBS 27:11	

Application:

1. How are you repeating the sins of your ancestors?
2. Do you feel that God is not hearing your requests? Ask the Spirit to search your heart for sin that might be hindering your communication with God.
3. Spend some time thanking God for providing Jesus to ransom you from your sins.
4. The sacrifice for our sins was accomplished forever through Christ. How are you denying Christ's sacrifice by attempting to earn salvation?
5. How has God revealed His goodness to you? Make a list of these and thank God for each one

EZEKIEL 21:1-22:31 HEBREWS 10:1-17 PSALM 108:1-13 PROVERBS 27:12	NOV **10**

Application:

1. Do you believe that God still judges sin? How does this impact the way you see the world?

2. The leaders of Israel allowed the nation to practice evil. Are your spiritual leaders warning you of the dangers of sin? Are you heeding the warnings? What warning signs in your life are you ignoring?

3. How can you prayerfully stand in the gap for the sinfulness of our society?

4. In response to Christ's sacrifice, we are called to give ourselves. How are you giving yourself to the cause of Christ?

5. Are God's laws written on your heart? What can you do to increase your understanding of God's expectations revealed in His law?

EZEKIEL 23:1-49 **HEBREWS 10:18-39** **PSALM 109:1-31** **PROVERBS 27:13**	**NOV** **11**

Application:

1. Even after God delivered Israel from Egypt, they continued to practice the idolatry committed in Egypt. Which idols are you still worshipping?
2. God is too big to be hidden behind your back. When do you attempt to exclude God from the activities of your life?
3. How does the blood of Christ give you confidence to enter God's presence?
4. What causes you to doubt God's salvation?
5. Who can you encourage with love and good deeds?
6. What hinders your perseverance in faith?

_____

_____

_____

_____

_____

_____

_____

EZEKIEL 24:1-26:21 HEBREWS 11:1-16 PSALM 110:1-7 PROVERBS 27:14	NOV **12**

Application:

1. Sin does not go unnoticed by God. Do you have "secret" sins that you pretend God doesn't see? Take time to confess these sins.

2. How do you yearn for the city that God is preparing? How do you live for the temporary experiences of this life?

3. Who are your Heroes of Faith? If they are still living, encourage them with a card or call today.

4. Would your faith qualify you for the Faith Hall of Fame? Spend some time today pondering this question. Ask God to help you grow in faith.

_____

_____

_____

_____

_____

_____

_____

EZEKIEL 27:1-28:26 HEBREWS 11:17-31 PSALM 111:1-10 PROVERBS 27:15-16	NOV **13**

Application:

1. God speaks against the arrogance of Tyre. The nation assumed that its national strength would keep it safe. How is your country guilty of such arrogance? Spend some time in prayer today for your country.

2. Abraham trusted God, the Promiser, more than he trusted the Promise. How do you differentiate between trusting the Promiser and trusting the Promise?

3. Joseph instructed Israel to carry his bones to the Promised Land. That command provided hope for Israel in dark days. What legacy are you leaving for your family?

4. Rahab's notation in the Faith Hall of Fame seems a bit out of place. Why do you think God included her name? How does her inclusion encourage you?

5. Do you quarrel with your spouse? How can you restrain your emotion and improve your communication?

EZEKIEL 29:1-30:26	NOV
HEBREWS 11:32-12:13	
PSALM 112:1-10	**14**
PROVERBS 27:17	

Application:

1. Egypt was a constant safety net for Israel. The Israelites always assumed that Egypt could bail them out in times of trouble. Who or what is your Egypt? Who do you believe can save you from difficult times? Don't place your trust in anything or anyone above God.

2. The Faith Hall of Fame is filled with those who received abuse rather than applause on earth. How might you be called to accept abuse for the sake of Christ?

3. What hinders and entangles you in your race of faith?

4. How does your race of faith differ from others?

5. How is God disciplining you? How are you accepting His discipline?

EZEKIEL 31:1-32:32 HEBREWS 12:14-29 PSALM 113:1-114:8 PROVERBS 27:18-20	NOV **15**

Application:

1. World powers come and go. Egypt and Assyria were once great but God upset their kingdoms. Remember, the only eternal kingdom is the one initiated by Christ. How does your life bear testimony to your citizenship in God's kingdom?

2. Are you living in peace with all men? What can you do to "bury the hatchet" with your enemies?

3. When have you exchanged a blessing for a bowl of stew? (Hebrews 12:16-17) How might you be tempted to place the temporary things of this earth ahead of the eternal things of God?

4. Where are you ignoring the voice of God in your life?

5. Watch the sun rise or the sun set today and praise God, who controls the sun!

EZEKIEL 33:1-34:31 HEBREWS 13:1-25 PSALM 115:1-18 PROVERBS 27:21-22	NOV **16**

Application:

1. Like Ezekiel, you have been entrusted as a watchman. (Ezekiel 33:7) Are you warning those you know about eternity separated from God? Who could you warn today?
2. What steps do you need to take to live out your faith?
3. What does it mean to you that God is your Shepherd? (Ezekiel 34:11)
4. How is your life perverted by the love of money? (Hebrews 13:5)
5. How does the constancy of Christ, "Jesus Christ is the same yesterday and today and forever." (Hebrews 13:8), encourage you today?
6. How do you handle praise?

_____

_____

_____

_____

_____

_____

_____

| EZEKIEL 35:1-36:38
JAMES 1:1-18
PSALM 116:1-19
PROVERBS 27:23-27 | NOV
17 |

Application:

1. God promises that Israel will be restored. What parts of your life need God's restoration?
2. God did not restore Israel based on their goodness or righteousness. He restored Israel for the sake of His name. God is still zealous for His name. When do you mistakenly assume that God saves you for your inherent value?
3. How has God used trials to mature your faith? How is He using trials now to mature your faith?
4. "Every good and perfect gift is from above..." (James 1:17) Take a few moments to thank God for all that He has given you.
5. How are you taking care of your household, investing time and energy today to prepare for tomorrow?

| EZEKIEL 37:1-38:23
JAMES 1:19-2:17
PSALM 117:1-2
PROVERBS 28:1 | NOV
18 |

Application:

1. God can make dry bones live. What can He do in your life?
2. No nation can stand against God's power. Praise God for His power.
3. Are you quick to listen, slow to speak and slow to become angry? (James 1:19) Most of us reverse that Biblical mandate. Work diligently this week to listen closely and avoid anger.
4. How can you put God's Word into practice this week?
5. According to the description in James, is your religion pure and faultless? (James 1:27)
6. "...faith by itself, if it is not accompanied by action, is dead." (James 2:17) How does this reality impact your understanding of faith?

_____

_____

_____

_____

_____

_____

EZEKIEL 39:1-40:27 JAMES 2:18-3:18 PSALM 118:1-18 PROVERBS 28:2	NOV **19**

Application:

1. God's punishment always has a purpose. He desires to bring His people back to Himself. Are you receiving God's punishment today? Repent and seek restoration.
2. How is your tongue an instrument of evil? How is your tongue an instrument of encouragement?
3. How does the way you speak to man reveal what you think of God?
4. Where in your life are you guided by selfish ambition?
5. How can you serve as a peacemaker in your sphere of influence?

_____

_____

_____

_____

_____

_____

| EZEKIEL 40:28-41:26
JAMES 4:1-17
PSALM 118:19-29
PROVERBS 28:3-5 | NOV
20 |

Application:

1. Ezekiel's vision of the Temple was a vision of hope. Israel was in exile, separated from the land and from God. The Temple was in ruins. God gave Ezekiel a vision of the Temple restored. How is God giving you a vision of a restored life, family, or church?

2. Have you considered that your internal ambition might be the cause of your external conflicts? What is God trying to change in you?

3. If we turn from the world and turn to God, He promises to draw near to us. How are you drawing near to God, earnestly seeking His face?

4. When do you attempt to usurp God's authority as a judge? Leave the role of judge in God's hands. (His omniscience makes Him far more qualified!)

5. Are you taking life for granted? Take time today to contemplate the gift of life. Ask God to protect you from taking your life for granted.

EZEKIEL 42:1-43:27	NOV
JAMES 5:1-20	
PSALM 119:1-16	**21**
PROVERBS 28:6-7	

Application:

1. Take a few moments to envision God filling the Temple, as described by Ezekiel. (Ezekiel 43:5) When are you tempted to become so familiar with God that you lose sight of His splendor?

2. How are you using the material resources God has given you to assist others in need?

3. Has your prayer life grown stale? Try praising God, confessing your sins, and sharing your prayer concerns with others.

4. How can you turn a sinner from error without being judgmental?

5. When do you measure your life by your bank account?

_____

_____

_____

_____

_____

_____

EZEKIEL 44:1-45:12 1 PETER 1:1-12 PSALM 119:17-32 PROVERBS 28:8-10	NOV **22**

Application:

1. Ezekiel is overwhelmed by the glory of God. When was the last time you were overwhelmed by God's glory? What caused it?

2. How do your daily actions match your Sunday sacrifices?

3. How does it make you feel to discover that you have been chosen by God?

4. How are your current trials proving your faith?

5. How does the promise of salvation impact your daily life?

| EZEKIEL 45:13-46:24
1 PETER 1:13-2:10
PSALM 119:33-48
PROVERBS 28:11 | NOV
23 |

Application:

1. God commands Israel to continue their feasts and festivals because these events reminded the people of God's activity. What do you do to remind yourself and your family of God's activity?
2. Would others describe you as self-controlled? Why or why not?
3. How do you strive for holiness on a daily basis?
4. The church is comprised of living stones. (1 Peter 2:5) What is your role as a living stone?
5. How does your life declare God's praises? (1 Peter 2:9)

EZEKIEL 47:1-48:35
1 PETER 2:11-3:7
PSALM 119:49-64
PROVERBS 28:12-13

NOV
24

Application:

1. God's instructions to Ezekiel on the division of the land might seem inconsequential to us. However, the instructions reinforce God's promise of return from exile. Are you longing for your eternal inheritance as Israel longed for the Land of Promise? What can you do to increase your anticipation of your eternal inheritance?

2. Could your church, your home or your city be given the label, The Lord is There? Why or why not?

3. Which sinful desires do you have the most difficulty abstaining from?

4. Where do you have trouble accepting authority? Remember that your attitude toward authority reveals your attitude toward God.

5. Do you spend as much time on your inner beauty as you spend on your outer beauty? What can you do to spend more time cultivating your inner beauty?

6. Concealed sin eats your soul like cancer. Confess your sin today and receive mercy.

DANIEL 1:1-2:23 **1 PETER 3:8-4:6** **PSALM 119:65-80** **PROVERBS 28:14**	**NOV** **25**

Application:

1. Daniel and the others obeyed God in the midst of exile. Are you out of your comfort zone? Ask God to help you as you continue to seek Him.

2. Daniel displayed tact and wisdom. How do your words display tact? How do your lips provide wisdom?

3. Do you have trouble living in harmony with certain people? Pray for those people today.

4. Is Christ the Lord of your life? How does His Lordship shine through your speech and actions?

5. What sinful habits has God removed from your life? Thank God for removing the destructive elements from your life.

_____

_____

_____

_____

_____

_____

DANIEL 2:24-3:30 1 PETER 4:7-5:14 PSALM 119:81-96 PROVERBS 28:15-16	NOV **26**

Application:

1. Daniel credited God with his ability to interpret the dream. (Daniel 2:45) When are you tempted to take credit for God's activity in your life?

2. The statue in Nebuchadnezzar's dream foretold of the kingdoms that would follow. Consider this; God is never surprised by the future! How does this encourage you today?

3. Shadrach, Meshach and Abednego trusted that God could save them but they were willing to stand boldly for God even if He did not save them. Pray that God will strengthen Christians who are persecuted for their faith.

4. Peter commands the Christians to love deeply. What would it look like for you to love your family deeply? Your church family? Your neighbors?

5. How does your life reflect true humility?

6. What burdens are you bearing that need to be handed over to Christ?

| DANIEL 4:1-37
2 PETER 1:1-21
PSALM 119:97-112
PROVERBS 28:17-18 | NOV
27 |

Application:

1. Nebuchadnezzar sent a letter to his people proclaiming God's activity in His life. Make an announcement today applauding God's activity in your life. Call a friend, post a message, or send an email.

2. In what areas do you need God to strengthen your spiritual life? Faith? Goodness? Knowledge? Self-control? Perseverance? Godliness? Brotherly kindness? Love?

3. What will it be like to receive the welcome of Christ in the eternal kingdom?

4. How does it change your approach to the Bible when you consider that Scripture is not the opinion of man but the Word of God?

5. Pray today's section of Psalm 119.

DANIEL 5:1-31 2 PETER 2:1-22 PSALM 119:113-128 PROVERBS 28:19-20	NOV **28**

Application:

1. Daniel was often forced to convey difficult messages. Pray that God would provide boldness when you are called on to share challenging messages.

2. Belshazzar's life displayed opulence and arrogance. The writing on the wall revealed that Belshazzar's arrogance was not overlooked by God. In what ways are you arrogant?

3. How can you recognize false prophets? How do you know if a messenger is from God or not?

4. Peter speaks of the false teachers as "experts in greed." Marketers today play on the greed of our sinful human nature. When have you succumbed to greed? How can you protect yourself against greed?

5. How can you prohibit daydreams from interrupting your work day?

DANIEL 6:1-28 2 PETER 3:1-18 PSALM 119:129-152 PROVERBS 28:21-22	NOV 29

Application:

1. Daniel's enemies could find no fault in Daniel's work. How would your enemies at work attack you? Ask God to help you display integrity at work so that you can glorify Him.

2. Daniel was in exile, separated from his land and his God, yet he continued to seek God in prayer. What types of exile threaten your communication with God?

3. Make a list of moments when God has rescued you. Share that list with your family or coworker today.

4. Peter wanted to stimulate his readers to "wholesome thinking." What thoughts deter you from wholesome thinking? Commit your thought life to God and ask Him to protect you from unwholesome thoughts.

5. What factors are hindering your spiritual growth? What factors are helping your spiritual growth?

_____

_____

_____

_____

_____

DANIEL 7:1-28 1 JOHN 1:1-10 PSALM 119:153-176 PROVERBS 28:23-24	NOV **30**

Application:

1. Daniel sees the Ancient of Days (God) interacting with one who is like a son of man (Jesus). The one like a son of man is given everlasting dominion. The day will come when the kingdoms of this earth will pass away and God's Kingdom will reign forever. Spend time today praising God for the kingdom that will be.

2. John wrote to give testimony of Christ. Who needs to hear a testimony about Jesus from your lips? Pray that God will give you opportunity and courage to testify of Christ.

3. What sins need to be confessed to God today so that you can enjoy His forgiveness?

4. Who has helped you by providing constructive criticism instead of flattery? Contact at least one of those individuals and thank them.

_____

_____

_____

_____

_____

_____

WHAT NOW?

December

DANIEL 8:1-27 1 JOHN 2:1-17 PSALM 120:1-7 PROVERBS 28:25-26	DEC **1**

Application:

1. Daniel's vision revealed events that have been confirmed in history. How does it make you feel to know that God knows the future?

2. Walking as Jesus walked is an impossible task in our own strength. Ask God to give you strength and wisdom as you seek to follow Jesus with your life.

3. How does the love of the world threaten to distract you in your walk with Christ? What precautions can you take to avoid these distractions?

4. Think about decisions that you have made over the last year. Which decisions were made in God's wisdom and which were made in your own strength? What precautions can you take to increase Godly wisdom in future decisions?

| DANIEL 9:1-11:1
1 JOHN 2:18-3:6
PSALM 121:1-8
PROVERBS 28:27-28 | DEC
2 |

Application:

1. Daniel engages in corporate confession as he laments over Israel's sin. Spend some time today in corporate confession. Acknowledge the sins of your family, your church, and your nation.

2. God promises eternal life. Spend some time thanking God for the eternal life that you will receive in Christ.

3. How does it make you feel to know that you are a child of God? Meditate on that truth today.

4. Praise God today for the help that He has given you this past week.

5. Who is in need around you? Ask God to open your eyes to see the needs around you.

_____

_____

_____

_____

_____

_____

DANIEL 11:2-35	DEC
1 JOHN 3:7-24	**3**
PSALM 122:1-9	
PROVERBS 29:1	

Application:

1. What or who threatens to lead you astray? (False teachers? Media? Selfish ambitions? Etc.?)
2. What hinders you from loving others?
3. Christ laid down His life for us. Reflect on the example of love given by Christ. Praise Him for this incredible sacrifice.
4. Ask God to reveal tangible actions that can show God's love to those around you.

DANIEL 11:36-12:13 1 JOHN 4:1-21 PSALM 123:1-4 PROVERBS 29:2-4	DEC **4**

Application:

1. God's knowledge of the future is not limited. He is in control of the end just as He was in control of the beginning. Meditate on the eternity that God promises to those who follow Him.

2. How do you test the messages you hear to discern if they are from God?

3. The one who is in you is greater than the one who is in the world. How does this knowledge impact your spiritual life?

4. Where has hatred crept into your life? How are you nursing hatred and allowing it to cripple your spiritual growth?

5. How has love cast out your fears?

_____

_____

_____

_____

_____

_____

HOSEA 1:1-3:5 1 JOHN 5:1-21 PSALM 124:1-8 PROVERBS 29:5-8	DEC 5

Application:

1. It is easy for us to downplay the effects of sin, but God compares Israel's sinfulness and idolatry to adultery. How does this comparison change your perception of sin?

2. Hosea's willingness to purchase his adulterous wife reveals God's grace for sinners. Spend some time thanking God for redeeming you from slavery to sin through Christ.

3. Obedience certainly isn't easy, so what does John mean when he says that the commands of Christ are not burdensome?

4. Those who do not have the Son of God do not have eternal life. How does this knowledge motivate you to tell others about Jesus? Pray that God will provide opportunities for you to testify of God's love in Christ.

5. Which idols distract you from Christ?

HOSEA 4:1-5:15 2 JOHN 1:1-13 PSALM 125:1-5 PROVERBS 29:9-11	DEC 6

Application:

1. The situation that Hosea addresses sounds eerily similar to contemporary culture: lying, murder, stealing and adultery. Pray that God would intervene in your community and in your country. Ask God to reveal ways that you can engage the sin of society with the Gospel.

2. The actions of Israel prohibited them from worshipping God. Ask God to expose any sinful behavior in your life that might be keeping you from connecting with God.

3. Think about the people in your life. Who is "walking in the truth" (2 John 1:4) or walking "in love" (2 John 1:6)? Encourage those individuals with a card or phone call.

4. John desired to interact face to face with the recipients of his letter. We have a myriad of methods to communicate, but the best method remains face to face communication. Who do you need to visit with face to face? Perhaps to resolve a conflict or renew a friendship? Schedule time to connect with that person.

5. What steps can you take to keep your anger under control? Start by asking for God's help!

HOSEA 6:1-9:17
3 JOHN 1:1-14
PSALM 126:1-6
PROVERBS 29:12-14

DEC

7

Application:

1. How can you show mercy to the people around you today?

2. What can you do to acknowledge God outside the walls of the church?

3. You might have heard the familiar expression, "You always reap what you sow." Did you know that this expression derived from the Bible? (Hosea 8:7) What are you reaping? What harvest will result from your current course of action?

4. The early church depended on hospitality. Who could benefit from your hospitality? Invite someone over for a meal or plan to eat out with some Christian friends or some friends who need Christ.

5. Gossip can infect the church. If you engage in gossip, ask God's forgiveness and His strength to overcome this habit. If you do not engage in gossip, be willing to stop those who do by refusing to listen.

HOSEA 10:1-14:9 JUDE 1:1-25 PSALM 127:1-5 PROVERBS 29:15-17	DEC 8

Application:

1. God wanted Israel to bless the nations but instead they focused inwardly. The same temptation exists for Christians today. How can you reveal God's blessing by blessing others?

2. Through Hosea, God reminds Israel that He is their God, the one who delivered them from Egypt. Israel's idolatry reveals that they had forgotten their deliverer. What can you do to remind yourself of the deliverance that you have received in Christ?

3. In what areas are you tempted to exchange grace for immorality? Ask God to help you experience His grace by resisting temptation.

4. When do you tend to grumble and find fault? Seek God's strength to handle those situations with patience.

JOEL 1:1-3:21	DEC
REVELATION 1:1-20	
PSALM 128:1-6	9
PROVERBS 29:18	

Application:

1. Israel was instructed to cry out to God in the face of judgment. Cry out to God today on behalf of those who are far from Him.

2. Even as God warns Israel of impending judgment, He extends grace. Who do you know that needs to hear about God's grace? Share with them about the God who is "gracious and compassionate, slow to anger and abounding in love." (Joel 2:13)

3. "Look, he is coming..." (Revelation 1:7) From the beginning, the book of Revelation points to the return of Christ. How does the imminent return of Christ impact your life? How should the imminent return of Christ impact your life?

4. The Revelation reminds us of Christ's dominion over this earth. As you read, write down the names given to Christ and the descriptions of Christ. Then, write about how those names impact your understanding of Jesus.

_____

_____

_____

_____

| AMOS 1:1-3:15
REVELATION 2:1-17
PSALM 129:1-8
PROVERBS 29:19-20 | DEC
10 |

Application:

1. Amos proclaimed judgment on the surrounding nations, which must have drawn approval from Israel. Then, he announced God's judgment on Israel. It is always easier to see sin in the lives of others. Ask God to make your sins apparent, so that you can confess them and receive His forgiveness.

2. Do you remember the fervor that you had for Christ, when you discovered His grace? How can you maintain the enthusiasm of that "first love?" (Revelation 2:4)

3. The message to the church in Smyrna is "Be faithful" and "Do not be afraid." (Revelation 2:10) Perhaps you are facing difficult times and you need the same exhortation.

4. Have you ever ignored sin for the sake of unity? While confrontation can be difficult, God's people must hold one another accountable. Pray that God will give you courage to confront sinful behavior and the humility to accept confrontation.

| AMOS 4:1-6:14
REVELATION 2:18-3:6
PSALM 130:1-8
PROVERBS 29:21-22 | DEC
11 |

Application:

1. Israel had slipped into an attitude of entitlement. What do you feel entitled to? Do your entitlements result in the oppression of others?

2. In addition to entitlement, Israel is rebuked for complacency. How has God pricked your heart to get involved with His mission? Ask for God's help to overcome your complacency.

3. Jesus promises rewards to those who overcome. Faith requires perseverance. Don't stop. Regardless of the obstacles, the destination is worthwhile.

4. Some at the church in Sardis were coasting in their faith and were on the verge of atrophy. Do you have areas of your faith that are decaying from lack of exercise? What can you do to stimulate growth in these areas?

AMOS 7:1-9:15 REVELATION 3:7-22 PSALM 131:1-3 PROVERBS 29:23	DEC **12**

Application:

1. Amos was not a prophet by vocation, he was a shepherd. However, when God revealed this message to Amos, he shared it. What is God calling you to do that might be outside your comfort zone or your experience?

2. Some in Israel attended worship while plotting to cheat their neighbors. Do you ever find yourself going through the motions of worship? What can you do to remain engaged in worship?

3. How can you tell when Christians are lukewarm? What signs accompany apathy?

4. Jesus offers to dine with His people. The meal was considered a time of fellowship and relationship-building. Plan a time this week when you can spend some extended time in prayer, seeking to cultivate your relationship with Christ.

_____

_____

_____

_____

_____

| OBADIAH 1:1-21
REVELATION 4:1-11
PSALM 132:1-18
PROVERBS 29:24-25 | DEC
13 |

Application:

1. Edom had profited from God's judgment on Israel. Through Obadiah, God warns the gloating Edomites that they will one day experience punishment. God supersedes national powers. Think back over the empires that have reigned since the time of Christ. Praise God for His sovereignty in every era. Also, praise God that He is still in control.

2. John witnessed a heavenly worship scene. Imagine that you are enjoying John's view. Use the words of the living creatures and the elders to inspire your own song of praise to the King of Kings.

3. In which areas of your life do you fear man? When do you worry about the opinions of others? How can you trust God in those areas? Ask the Holy Spirit to direct you as you seek to trust God.

JONAH 1:1-4-11 REVELATION 5:1-14 PSALM 133:1-3 PROVERBS 29:26-27	DEC **14**

Application:

1. God wanted to extend grace to Nineveh and use Jonah in the process. God still wants to extend grace today and He wants to use you in the process. How is God using you to extend His grace? Who are you uniquely equipped to reach?

2. Jonah's story is not only a story of sending, it is also a story of receiving. God gave you His grace. Spend some time today praising God for His incredible gift of grace.

3. Jesus is the lamb that was slain for the sins of man. Thank God for giving you the gift that you could never obtain.

4. "Worthy is the lamb." (Revelation 5:12) Make a list of 10 reasons that Jesus is worthy of praise. Share at least two items from your list with someone today.

5. Are you looking for an earthly court to give you justice? Remember, true justice only comes from the Lord.

MICAH 1:1-4:13	DEC
REVELATION 6:1-17	**15**
PSALM 134:1-3	
PROVERBS 30:1-4	

Application:

1. The people of Judah were experiencing economic prosperity when Micah proclaimed his message of impending judgment. The people didn't believe Micah's warning. External circumstances are not always accurate indicators of an internal spiritual condition. Take some time today to do an honest assessment of your spiritual health.

2. Micah provides hope in the midst of judgment. He speaks of a time when people will exchange weapons of war for farming equipment. Praise God for the peace that He provides and especially for the peace He will provide in the future.

3. While the reading from Revelation tempts us to speculate on the meaning of the four riders, we should concentrate on the dominion of God. Notice the fear of the people as they face the one who sits on the throne. Ask God to remind you of His dominion throughout the day. Look for situations and circumstances that reveal that God is in control.

| MICAH 5:1-7:20
REVELATION 7:1-17
PSALM 135:1-21
PROVERBS 30:5-6 | DEC
16 |

Application:

1. Through Micah, God asks the people of Israel, "How have I burdened you?" (Micah 6:3) Do you look on your faith as a burden? Why or why not? How could you change your perspective on your faith?

2. God desires for His people to walk humbly with him. How are you walking with God today? What could you change to strengthen that walk?

3. The multi-ethnic group of worshippers depicted in Revelation reminds us that Christ's kingdom extends to all nations. What can you do to spread the gospel to the nations? What can you do to increase fellowship with Christians of other ethnic backgrounds?

4. What do you think heaven will be like? How does your image fit with the depiction in John's Revelation?

NAHUM 1:1-3:19 REVELATION 8:1-13 PSALM 136:1-26 PROVERBS 30:7-9	DEC **17**

Application:

1. The city of Nineveh repented when they received the reluctant message of Jonah. A century later they refused to repent when confronted by Nahum. Sometimes we grow comfortable in our sin and refuse to repent. What sin is God calling you to confess?

2. Do you need to seek God as a refuge today? Acknowledge your dependence on God and ask for His strength.

3. Many ask how a good God could judge sinners. God has the power to destroy the earth and all within the earth. Perhaps we would do better to ask how a Holy God allows humanity to exist! Thank God today for His gentleness.

4. Make a list of the moments in your life when God's power was evident. After each item record the reminder of the Psalmist, "His love endures forever."

_____

_____

_____

_____

_____

_____

| HABAKKUK 1:1–3:19 REVELATION 9:1-21 PSALM 137:1-9 PROVERBS 30:10 | DEC 18 |

Application:

1. The people question God's silence and discover that God was working all along to bring about His purpose. Are you struggling with the silence of God? If so, find strength in the reality that God is still in control. Bring your concerns to God today, revealing that you are not afraid of His silence.

2. What deeds of God stir awe and wonder in you? Express your worship to God in prayer or song.

3. John noted that even those in his vision that faced great tribulation refused to acknowledge their sin. What sins are you hiding from the searching gaze of Christ? Repent of those sins and receive God's forgiveness.

| ZEPHANIAH 1:1-3:20
REVELATION 10:1-11
PSALM 138:1-8
PROVERBS 30:11-14 | DEC
19 |

Application:

1. Zephaniah promises that the "day of the LORD" is coming. (Zephaniah 1:14) Are you ready for the "day of the LORD"?

2. Imagine what it will look like for God to "quiet you with his love" and "rejoice over you with singing." (Zephaniah 3:17) Live today in light of that future reality.

3. God's mystery will be accomplished. We know the conclusion to the story. Ask God to help you live each day in light of the culmination that is coming.

4. John was called to share the message he received on Patmos. What is God calling you to share with your family and friends? A message of hope? A message of encouragement? A word of warning?

_____

_____

_____

_____

_____

_____

HAGGAI 1:1-2:23 REVELATION 11:1-19 PSALM 139:1-24 PROVERBS 30:15-16	DEC **20**

Application:

1. After returning from exile, the Israelites delayed rebuilding the Lord's Temple. They claimed that the timing wasn't right, but in reality they didn't want to divert their personal resources to the building project. What tempts you to hold back what rightfully belongs to God?

2. God used Haggai and Zerubbabel as leaders in the building project. What is God calling you to lead in your community of faith? What is God calling you to initiate in your community?

3. The scene depicted in Revelation 11 reminds us of God's power. God has power over all nations and people. Meditate on God's power for a few moments and then write out a prayer of praise to your All-Powerful God.

4. The Psalmist reminds us that God knows our thoughts. When do your thoughts glorify God? When do your thoughts dishonor God? Ask God to help you take your thoughts captive.

| ZECHARIAH 1:1-21
REVELATION 12:1-17
PSALM 140:1-13
PROVERBS 30:17 | DEC
21 |

Application:

1. Like Haggai, Zechariah prophesied after the exile. The people were excited about the return to Israel but they were still frightened. God's message through Zechariah promises hope. God still spreads hope to His people. Ask God to rekindle your hope.

2. Revelation depicts a cosmic battle between God and Satan. This battle rages beyond our senses. In Ephesians 6:12, Paul reminds us that our battle is "not against flesh and blood." Ask God to increase your awareness of this cosmic battle. Make a point to pray for the supernatural events that occur outside your ability to comprehend.

3. How can you show obedience and honor to your parents?

_____

_____

_____

_____

_____

_____

ZECHARIAH 2:1-3:10 REVELATION 13:1-18 PSALM 141:1-10 PROVERBS 30:18-20	DEC **22**

Application:

1. God promised His protection and His presence to those who returned to Israel from Babylon. He offers the same to you today. How do you need God's protection? How do you need His presence?

2. Zechariah prophesies of Jesus, whom he calls the Branch. How is Jesus a Branch? What does that name reveal to you about the Messiah?

3. The Psalmist seeks the Lord's presence through prayer. In your prayer life, do you truly seek God's presence? If not, what attitudes need to change in your prayer life? What practices could be altered to make your prayer life more personal?

4. The adulteress denies wrongdoing. Do you have sins that you refuse to acknowledge?

ZECHARIAH 4:1-5:11	DEC
REVELATION 14:1-20	**23**
PSALM 142:1-7	
PROVERBS 30:21-23	

Application:

1. Zerubbabel was called to lead the people to rebuild God's Temple. This was an enormous task and God assured Zechariah that the task would only be completed by the Lord's power. What are you attempting that can only be accomplished by God's power?

2. The 144,000 who are seen with the lamb are said to be blameless. Though we are cleansed of sin by the blood of Christ, we are still called to strive for Holiness. What hinders you from being blameless? Ask God to help you to live blamelessly before Him.

3. David cried out in desperation to God. What do you need to take to God in prayer?

4. The dead in Christ will rest from their labor. At times we grow weary in service, but God offers us rest in the future. Ask God to strengthen you today with the promise of rest in the future.

_____

_____

_____

_____

_____

ZECHARIAH 6:1-7:14 REVELATION 15:1-8 PSALM 143:1-12 PROVERBS 30:24-28	DEC **24**

Application:

1. The Lord rebukes Israel for ritualistic religion that refused to show mercy in the real world. They fasted and prayed but failed to show mercy and compassion. How do you express your faith in the real world? What can you do to insure that your spiritual disciplines facilitate action?

2. While the description of the dragon and the beast in John's Revelation might cause concern, the Revelation reminds us that Christ is victorious over all opposition. How does Christ's victory impact your life?

3. Join David in this prayer: "Teach me to do your will, for you are my God." (Psalm 143:10)

4. The ant provides a picture of industriousness. Contemporary culture seems to breed entitlement over industriousness. Which best describes you? How can you alter your habits to be more industrious?

_____

_____

_____

_____

_____

| ZECHARIAH 8:1-23
REVELATION 16:1-21
PSALM 144:1-15
PROVERBS 30:29-31 | DEC
25 |

Application:

1. Zechariah promises a time of revival and renewal in Israel. Pray that God will send revival and renewal to your church and to your community?

2. One angel commented that God's judgment was just. How is God just in His judgment?

3. Repeatedly, the Revelation calls believers to be prepared for Christ's return and judgment. Are you prepared? What do you need to do to live prepared?

4. In the opening lines of Psalm 144, David refers to God as his rock, fortress, stronghold, deliverer, shield, and refuge. Think of five terms that you would use to describe God.

_____

_____

_____

_____

_____

_____

| ZECHARIAH 9:1-17
REVELATION 17:1-18
PSALM 145:1-21
PROVERBS 30:32 | DEC
26 |

Application:

1. God promises destruction on those who oppress Israel and restoration for His chosen people. Who or what oppresses you? Rejoice because God will overcome your oppressors.

2. The image-laden language of the Revelation reminds us that God will overcome the principalities of this world. What world powers or movements concern you? What cultural ideologies discourage you? Remember that God rules over all on this earth. Praise Him for He is in control.

3. Use Psalm 145 as a prayer to God.

4. Ask God to halt any evil plans or evil words that might originate in you.

_____

_____

_____

_____

_____

_____

| ZECHARIAH 10:1-11:17
REVELATION 18:1-24
PSALM 146:1-10
PROVERBS 30:33 | DEC
27 |

Application:

1. Through Zechariah, God promises restoration for Israel. God is still in the business of restoration. Spend a few moments thanking God for the areas of your life that He has restored. Also submit to Him the areas that still need His restoring touch.

2. Babylon symbolized the Roman Empire. Even the mighty Roman Empire was no match for the power and authority of God. As you consider current world powers, remember that God's authority exceeds all others. Pray for God's will to be done today in global politics.

3. How can you join God in His work of watching over the alien and sustaining the fatherless and the widow?

4. Who has a unique ability to make you angry? Ask God to give you specific patience with that person. Who do you have the unique ability to make angry? Ask God to help you show grace to that person.

_____

_____

_____

_____

_____

ZECHARIAH 12:1-13:9	DEC
REVELATION 19:1-21	
PSALM 147:1-20	28
PROVERBS 31:1-7	

Application:

1. Zechariah foretells of a fountain that will offer forgiveness. That fountain is Christ. What sins do you need to bring to the fountain of forgiveness? Spend some time accepting God's grace.

2. The inhabitants of heaven praise the Lamb as a victorious conqueror. Do you praise Jesus as a victorious conqueror? Spend a few minutes praising Jesus as the conqueror of death.

3. Read the description of Jesus in Revelation 19 several times slowly. Develop a mental picture of the King of Kings and Lord of Lords. (If you are an artist, try to sketch the image.) Allow this image to direct your praise.

4. King Lemuel warns of the dangers of alcohol. (Proverbs 31:4) What substances, possessions, or obsessions are you allowing to misdirect your life?

| ZECHARIAH 14:1-21
REVELATION 20:1-15
PSALM 148:1-14
PROVERBS 31:8-9 | DEC
29 |

Application:

1. Zechariah points toward a day when God will once again rule over the entire earth. If God were physically ruling on earth, how would your life change?

2. The Revelation clearly tells the story of God's dominion over the devil. While Satan still attacks us, his authority and power never surpasses God's. If you sense that the devil is attacking you in a particular area, take that concern to Christ today.

3. Is your name written in the book of life? If so, rejoice and praise God for giving you life through His Son. If not, you can accept God's salvation today by acknowledging your sin, accepting God's grace, and submitting your life to God's authority.

4. Who is unable to speak up? Whose rights are being overlooked? How can you give a voice to their needs?

_____

_____

_____

_____

_____

MALACHI 1:1-2:17 REVELATION 21:1-27 PSALM 149:1-9 PROVERBS 31:10-24	DEC **30**

Application:

1. The priests and the people are rebuked for bringing their leftovers to God. As God's children and recipients of His grace, we should strive to give Him the very best of our lives. Do a quick evaluation; are there any areas of your life where you are giving God leftovers? If so, make plans to start giving God your best.

2. God checks to see if our words and our actions match. As the New Year approaches, what actions need to be brought in line with your words?

3. While the golden gates and jewel-laden walls sound appealing, the most exciting promise of heaven is that "…God himself will be with them and be their God." (Revelation 21:3) Praise God for His presence today and for His promised presence in heaven!

4. Allow your imagination to ponder heaven as described in Revelation 21: God's presence, no tears, no sin or impurity, etc.

5. Make a list of the characteristics of the Proverbs 31 woman. If you are a husband, affirm your wife in writing for the characteristics that she embodies. If you are a wife, thank God for giving you the characteristics you possess and ask God to give you those that are not yet apparent. If your mother is still living, write her a note expressing your appreciation.

| MALACHI 3:1-4:6
REVELATION 22:1-21
PSALM 150:1-6
PROVERBS 31:25-31 | DEC
31 |

Application:

1. God refines His people. If you are experiencing God's purification, rejoice for He is shaping you into His image.
2. Many struggle to trust God in the realm of finances. As a new year approaches, look closely at your finances and commit to honor God in your spending.
3. Praise God for the promise that one day the curse of sin will be removed.
4. Repeatedly Christ reminds that He is returning soon. How does the knowledge of Christ's imminent return impact your life?
5. Who do you know that is thirsty and needs to hear about the free gift of eternal water?

CPSIA information can be obtained
at www.ICGtesting.com
Printed in the USA
BVOW03s0221120117
473313BV00001B/10/P